REVISE BTEC NATIONAL
Art and Design

REVISION WORKBOOK

Series Consultant: Harry Smith

Authors: Daniel Freaker and Alan Parsons

A note from the publisher

While the publishers have made every attempt to ensure that advice on the qualification and its assessment is accurate, the official specification and associated assessment guidance materials are the only authoritative source of information and should always be referred to for definitive guidance.

This qualification is reviewed on a regular basis and may be updated in the future. Any such updates that affect the content of this Revision Workbook will be outlined at **www.pearsonfe.co.uk/BTECchanges**.

> **For the full range of Pearson revision titles across KS2, KS3, GCSE, Functional Skills, AS/A Level and BTEC visit:**
> www.pearsonschools.co.uk/revise

C334321142

Published by Pearson Education Limited, 80 Strand, London, WC2R 0RL.

www.pearsonschoolsandfecolleges.co.uk

Copies of official specifications for all Pearson qualifications may be found on the website: qualifications.pearson.com

Text and illustrations © Pearson Education Limited 2018
Typeset and illustrated by Kamae Design, Oxford
Produced by Out of House Publishing
Cover design by Miriam Sturdee

The rights of Daniel Freaker and Alan Parsons to be identified as authors of this work have been asserted by them in accordance with the Copyright, Designs and Patents Act 1988.

First published 2018

20 19 18
10 9 8 7 6 5 4 3 2 1

British Library Cataloguing in Publication Data
A catalogue record for this book is available from the British Library

ISBN 978 1 292 15007 9

Acknowledgements
The authors and publisher would like to thank the following individuals and organisations for their kind permission to reproduce copyright material.

Text
Page 004: From the Essay 'The Transformation of Silence into Language and Action' by Audre Lorde – Sister Outsider © 1984, 2007
Pages 089, 094, 094, 096, 096, 097, 097: Reproduced with the permission of Cancer Research UK.
Page 129: Reproduced with the permission of Cambridge University Press.

Please note that content in the revision brief on pages 87–98 is for illustrative purposes, and some content provided by Cancer Research UK has been amended by the Publisher for the purposes of the brief. Cancer Research UK is independent from Pearson Education Ltd and a source of trusted information for all. The use of content linked to Cancer Research UK does not indicate that Cancer Research UK directly endorses Pearson Education Ltd or its products and services. The Publisher extends thanks to Cancer Research UK for their kind permission.

Photographs
(Key: b-bottom; c-centre; l-left; r-right; t-top)

123RF: Zven0 5crb, Stockbroker 94b, Leaf 96c, Eraxion 130tl, 130cr; **Alamy Stock Photo:** PNC Collection 4cl, Jennifer Wright 4bl, Chris Dorney 4bcl, Tony French 5cl, UK Retail Alan King 5bl, Prisma by Dukas Presseagentur GmbH 17, Ray Allen 95b,

Alan Fraser 98t; **Alan Parsons:** Alan Parsons 115, 116, 150, 153; **Bridgeman Images:** War Paintings And Drawings at the Leicester Gallery, Leicester Square, London (colour litho), English School, (20th century)/Private Collection/Photo © Barbara Singer 4cbr, Spilliaert, Leon (1881-1946)/Private Collection/Photo © Christie's Images 10; **Bridgeman Images/DACS:** © Julian Schnabel/ARS, New York/DACS. Private Collection/Photo © Christie's Images/Bridgeman Images 7, © The Andy Warhol Foundation for the Visual Arts, Inc./DACS/Artimage 2018 62, © Ian Davenport. All Rights Reserved, DACS/Artimage 2018 71b; **Bridget Riley:** 'Movement in Squares', 1961, Tempera on hardboard, 123.2 x 121.2cm | 48 ½ × 47 ¾ Arts Council Collection, Southbank Centre, London. © 2016 Bridget Riley. All rights reserved. Courtesy Karsten Schubert, London 60; **Cancer Research UK:** 94t, 95t, 96b, 97c, **Daniel Freaker:** ©Daniel Freaker 16l, 16r, 25, 26, 29; **Gagosian Gallery:** © Michael Craig-Martin. Courtesy the artist and Gagosian. 9; **George Newton:** © George Newton 30, 38; **Getty Images:** UrsaHoogle 97t; **Jessie Major:** © Jessie Major 41; **Lauren Moncreaff:** © Lauren Moncreaff 22; **M.C. Escher:** M.C. Escher's "Symmetry Drawing E126" © 2018 The M.C. Escher Company-The Netherlands. All rights reserved. www.mcescher.com 59; **Megan Schneider:** © Megan Schneider 149; **Michael Brennand-Wood:** Michael Brennand-Wood - Visual Artist, Arts Consultant, Curator & Educator 71t; **Pearson Education Ltd:** Oxford Designers & Illustrators Ltd 129t, Coleman Yuen 130clb; **Rex Features:** PIXELFORMULA/SIPA/SIPA/REX/Shutterstock 5bc; **Shutterstock:** C Salisbury 4tl, Militarist 4tr, Esteban De Armas 4cr, Mark Hayes 4cbl, Dragunov 4bcr, Verena Matthew 4br, Sean Nel 5tl, Dan Tautan 5tcl, Scorpp 5tcr, Kuleczka 5tr, Paulaphoto 5cr, Pio3 5clb, Roxana Bashyrova 5brt, Lightspring 5br, Nicolo_Moioli_fotografia 15, VGstockstudio 18, Nadino 96t, Yulia Davidovich 96cl, Lisa S. 96cr, Vertes Edmond Mihai 97cl, Goodluz 97cr, Monkey Business Images 98b, A1Stock 129bl, Olaf Ludwig 129br, David Herraez Calzada 130tr, Eliane Haykal 130cl, Songsak P 130bl, Trekandshoot 130br;

All other images © Pearson Education

Websites
Pearson Education Limited is not responsible for the content of any external internet sites. It is essential for tutors to preview each website before using it in class so as to ensure that the URL is still accurate, relevant and appropriate. We suggest that tutors bookmark useful websites and consider enabling students to access them through the school/college intranet.

Notes from the publisher
1. While the publishers have made every attempt to ensure that advice on the qualification and its assessment is accurate, the official specification and associated assessment guidance materials are the only authoritative source of information and should always be referred to for definitive guidance. Pearson examiners have not contributed to any sections in this resource relevant to examination papers for which they have responsibility.

2. Pearson has robust editorial processes, including answer and fact checks, to ensure the accuracy of the content in this publication, and every effort is made to ensure this publication is free of errors. We are, however, only human, and occasionally errors do occur. Pearson is not liable for any misunderstandings that arise as a result of errors in this publication, but it is our priority to ensure that the content is accurate. If you spot an error, please do contact us at resourcescorrections@pearson.com so we can make sure it is corrected.

Introduction

Which units should you revise?

This Workbook has been designed to help you revise the skills you may need for the externally assessed units of your course. You won't necessarily be studying all the units included here – it will depend on the qualification you are taking.

BTEC Level 3 National Qualification	Externally assessed units
Certificate	1 Visual Recording and Communication
For both: Extended Certificate Foundation Diploma	1 Visual Recording and Communication 2 Critical and Contextual Studies in Art and Design
Diploma	1 Visual Recording and Communication 2 Critical and Contextual Studies in Art and Design 7 Developing and Realising Creative Intentions
For each of: Diploma P (Photography) Diploma G (Graphics) Diploma 3D (3D Design and Crafts) Diploma FD (Fashion Design and Production)	6 Managing a Client Brief 7 Developing and Realising Creative Intentions
Extended Diploma	1 Visual Recording and Communication 2 Critical and Contextual Studies in Art and Design 6 Managing a Client Brief 7 Developing and Realising Creative Intentions

Your Workbook

Each unit in this Workbook contains a set of revision tasks to help you **revise the skills** you may need in your assessment. The selected content, outcomes, questions and answers used in each unit are provided to help you to revise content and ways of applying your skills. Ask your tutor or check the Pearson website for the most up-to-date **Sample Assessment Material** and **Mark Schemes** to get an indication of the structure of your actual assessment and what this requires of you. The detail of the actual assessment may change so always make sure you are up to date.

This Workbook will often include one or more useful features that explain or break down longer questions or tasks. Remember that these features won't appear in your actual assessment!

> Grey boxes like this contain **hints and tips** about ways that you might complete a task, interpret a brief, understand a concept or structure your responses.

 Guided ▷ This icon will appear next to an **example partial answer** to a revision question or revision task. You should read the partial answer carefully, then complete it in your own words.

> This is a **revision activity**. It will help you understand some of the skills needed to complete the revision task or question.

> 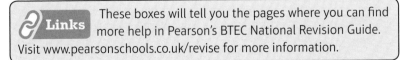 **Links** These boxes will tell you the pages where you can find more help in Pearson's BTEC National Revision Guide.
> Visit www.pearsonschools.co.uk/revise for more information.

There is often space on the pages of this Workbook for you to write in. However, if you are carrying out research and make ongoing notes, you may want to use separate paper. Similarly, some units may be assessed through submission of digital files, or on screen, rather than on paper. Ask your tutor or check the Pearson website for the most up-to-date details.

Contents

A small bit of small print

Pearson publishes Sample Assessment Material and the specification on its website. That is the official content, and this book should be used in conjunction with it. The revision questions and revision tasks in this book have been written to help you practise what you have learned in your revision. Remember: the real assessment may not look like this.

Unit 1: Visual Recording and Communication

Your set task

Unit 1 will be assessed through a task, which will be set by Pearson. You will need to use your understanding of investigating, experimenting and exploring a range of visual recording materials and methods to express and communicate ideas, as you carry out research and prepare a response to a provided theme. You will then complete a fully developed piece of art and design in response to the provided theme and produce a written commentary that explains and justifies your ideas and decisions.

Your Revision Workbook

This Workbook is designed to **revise skills** that you might need in your assessed task. The selected content, outcomes, questions and answers are provided to help you to revise content and ways of applying your skills. Ask your tutor or check the **Pearson website** for the most up-to-date **Sample Assessment Material** and **Mark Scheme** to get an indication of the structure of your actual assessed task and what this requires of you. Pay attention to requirements in relation to submission of images, any word limitation to written work, whether you have access to a computer, whether you can take any research and preparatory work into the supervised assessment and how much time you have for different parts of the task. The details of the actual assessed task may change so always make sure you are up to date.

1 **Research and prepare in response to a theme (pages 2–35)**

   - Read and respond to starting points on a specified theme.
   - Research and record work by art and design practitioners relevant to a theme.
   - Identify, research and record from relevant sources that relate to a theme (e.g. primary sources, including an observational recording; secondary sources; historical and contextual references).
   - Demonstrate visual communication of the theme in different ways (e.g. style, medium, technique, interpretation), documenting your research and exploration.

2 **Consider a fully developed piece of art or design that responds to a theme (pages 36–42)**

   - This may be an **extension** or **development** of work produced during the research and recording stage (see Research and prepare, above).
   - **Or** this may be a **stand-alone** piece of work informed by the research and development (see Research and prepare, above).

3 **Prepare for a written commentary (pages 43–50)**

4 **Respond to activities, showing your ability in visual recording and communication (pages 51–53)**

   - Consider how you would select work from the 'research and prepare' stage to mount and demonstrate the quality and breadth of your work.
   - Consider how you would mount a fully developed piece of art and design that demonstrates the quality and interpretation of your response to a theme, use of materials and communication of creative intentions.
   - Consider how you would produce a written commentary to accompany your mounted work, which includes explanations that show analysis of the use of visual language and formal elements in your own and others' work, quality and detail in explanation, and justifications for decisions made in your research and fully developed piece of art and design.

> **Links** To help you revise skills that might be needed in your Unit 1 assessed task, this Workbook contains a revision task starting on page 2. See the introduction on page iii for more information on features included to help you revise.

Revision task

To support your revision, this Workbook contains a revision task to help you **revise the skills** that you might need in your assessed task. Ask your tutor or check the Pearson website for the most up-to-date **Sample Assessment Material** and **Mark Scheme** to establish what is required of you. The details of the actual assessed task may change so always make sure you are up to date.

Revision task brief

Although you are given a revision brief that includes researching, producing and mounting pieces of art or design that respond to the theme 'Protection', the activities in this Workbook will only require you to focus on the skills associated with the tasks. You are **not** expected to undertake full research, preparation, production and mounting of a full piece of art or design and associated tasks. Although the theme in the revision brief is 'Protection', the activities in this Workbook may also involve a wider range of images to demonstrate skills that you can apply with any theme.

For this task you will produce a piece of art or design that responds to the theme 'Protection'.

A document is provided on pages 4–5 with a series of images, quotations, artists and designers that will provide the starting points for the development of your ideas.

You should explore the theme initially through contextual research, primary and observational recordings and secondary sources.

By completing this task, you will demonstrate you are able to:
- visually record from primary and secondary sources in response to a theme
- research and record work by art and design practitioners linked to the theme
- research and record own contextual influences and factors in response to a theme
- produce a fully developed piece of art or design that communicates the theme.

Research and preparatory stage

Before completing revision activities 1–3 you must undertake research and preparation.

Ask your tutor or check the up-to-date Sample Assessment Material on the Pearson website for how many hours you have for research and preparation in your actual assessment. Make sure you plan so that you complete the work within the allocated time. Pay attention to details, such as whether you can take work from your research stage into your assessed activities.

During this time, you must:
- research and record work by art and design practitioners relevant to a theme
- identify, research and record from relevant sources that relate to a theme. This may include:
  - primary sources
  - secondary sources
  - historical and contextual references.

You must ensure that:
- **at least one** of your records is an observational recording from a primary source
- you demonstrate visual communication of a theme in at least three different ways, for example through style, medium, technique, interpretation
- you document all your research and exploration of the materials and methods you have used throughout this stage.

Completion of fully developed piece

Once you have completed your research and preparatory stage you must produce **one fully developed piece of art or design** that responds to the theme.

This can be an extension and development of work produced during the research and recording stage or a stand-alone piece of work informed by the research and development.

Revision activities

Revision activity 1

Select from the research and preparatory stage to mount onto no more than three A2 presentation sheets.

The work you select should demonstrate:

- your ability to visually communicate the theme in different ways
- your exploration of ideas, imagery and visual language
- your exploration of materials and methods of recording
- at least one observational recording from a primary source
- your research into art and design practitioners
- the contextual factors you investigated.

Make sure you show:

- the quality of your research into art and design practitioners
- the quality and breadth of your visual recording and research
- your understanding and application of contextual factors linked to a theme.

Revision activity 2

Mount the work/images of your fully developed piece of art or design onto one presentation sheet of A2 paper.

The work produced should demonstrate:

- your response to a theme
- your use of materials, techniques and processes
- your ability to communicate your creative intentions.

Make sure you show:

- your interpretation and communication of a theme
- your ability to manipulate materials, techniques and processes to communicate your creative intentions.

Revision activity 3

Produce a written commentary to accompany the four A2 presentation sheets you have produced in Activity 1 and Activity 2. This should include explanations on:

- your interpretation of a theme
- the art and design practitioners you researched and how they influenced your work
- the primary and secondary sources you used in response to a theme
- the visual recording methods and material you used
- your own visual recording and communication in relation to a theme, including decisions made, strengths and weaknesses and areas for improvement in your own work.

Make sure you show:

- your analysis of the use of visual language and formal elements in your own and others' work
- the quality and detail in your explanations and justifications for decisions made.

> Although the revision task refers to completion and mounting of pieces of art and design for revision activities 1 and 2 and a written commentary for revision activity 3, this Workbook will only require you to focus on the associated skills within a practical revision timeframe. Ask your tutor or check the latest Sample Assessment Material on the Pearson website to establish what is required in your actual assessment and how many hours you have for your assessed activities so that you can complete them within the allocated time. Pay attention to any details such as the **size** and **number** of presentation sheets and whether there is a **word limit** for your commentary. Details of assessment may change, so always make sure you are up to date.

Revision task information

This revision task information is used as an example to show the skills you need. The content of a task will be different each year and the format may be different. Ask your tutor or check the latest Sample Assessment Material on the Pearson website for more details.

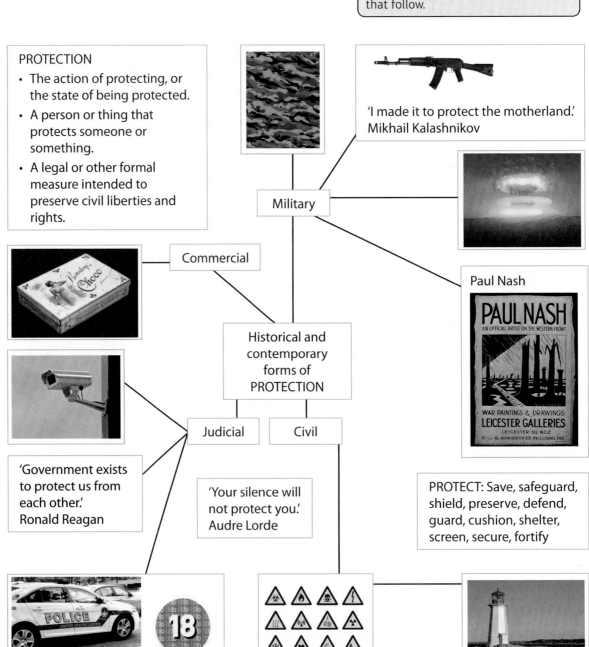

PROTECTION

You have been asked to explore and investigate the theme 'Protection' to produce creative outcomes. The theme should be seen as a starting point and you should explore appropriate primary and secondary sources and contextual material.

Possible starting points

This is not an exhaustive and definitive list and should be seen as possible inspiration start points.

Start by carefully reading the series of images, quotes, artists and designers that follow.

PROTECTION
- The action of protecting, or the state of being protected.
- A person or thing that protects someone or something.
- A legal or other formal measure intended to preserve civil liberties and rights.

'I made it to protect the motherland.'
Mikhail Kalashnikov

Military

Commercial

Paul Nash

PAUL NASH
AN OFFICIAL ARTIST ON THE WESTERN FRONT

WAR PAINTINGS & DRAWINGS
LEICESTER GALLERIES
LEICESTER SQ. W.C.2
10 TILL 6. ADMISSION 1/3 INCLUDING TAX

Historical and contemporary forms of PROTECTION

Judicial

Civil

'Government exists to protect us from each other.'
Ronald Reagan

'Your silence will not protect you.'
Audre Lorde

PROTECT: Save, safeguard, shield, preserve, defend, guard, cushion, shelter, screen, secure, fortify

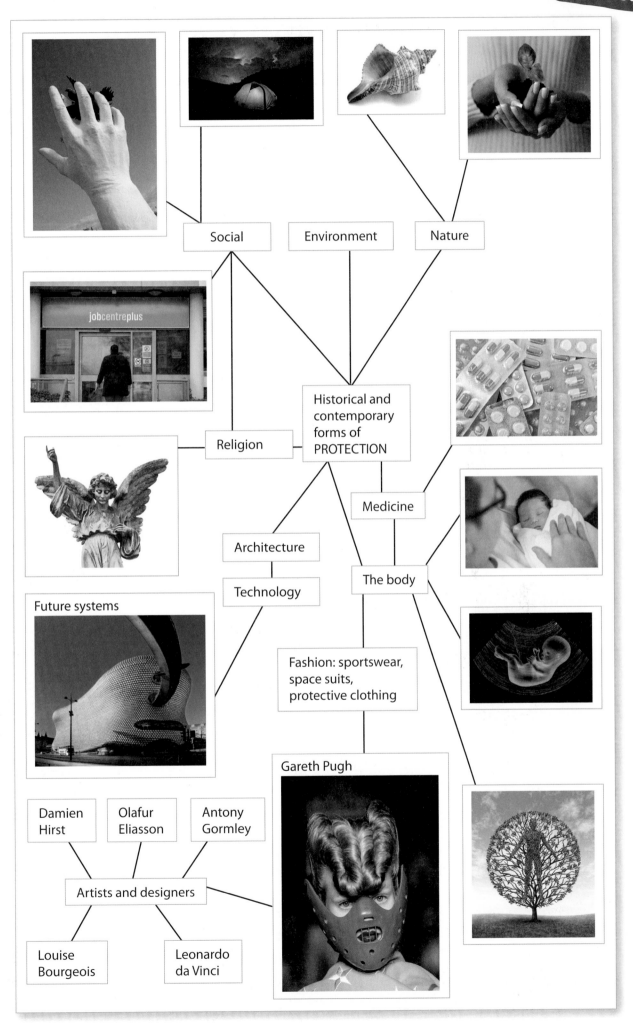

Social

Environment

Nature

jobcentreplus

Historical and contemporary forms of PROTECTION

Religion

Medicine

Architecture

The body

Technology

Future systems

Fashion: sportswear, space suits, protective clothing

Gareth Pugh

| Damien Hirst | Olafur Eliasson | Antony Gormley |

Artists and designers

| Louise Bourgeois | Leonardo da Vinci |

Interpreting a brief

When **reading** and **responding** to starting points on a specified theme such as 'Protection' in order to produce a piece of art or design, consider the **requirements of the brief**.

Guided **1** Complete the mind map of themed ideas for possible areas of exploration.

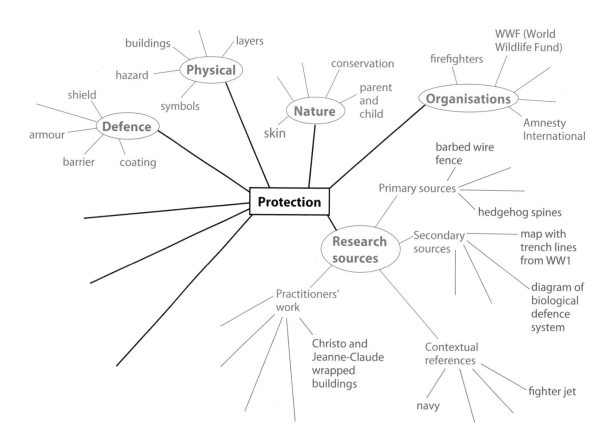

> **Primary sources**: direct observational recording
>
> **Secondary sources**: internet, books, magazines, journals, film, photographs, animation, video, music, audio
>
> **Contextual factors**: time or era the work was produced within, or any political, social or cultural influences

2 Note your choices as an initial response to the brief. Bear in mind research, recording and ideas generation.

(a) What are your first thoughts for a piece of art and design that connect with starting points of the theme and reflect your own specialism and interests?

....

(b) What are your first thoughts for researching and recording from art and design practitioners' work, and primary, secondary, historical and contextual sources?

....

(c) How do you plan to document your range of research, visual recording and notes?

....

(d) How will you plan your time between researching/recording and producing a fully developed piece?

....

> **Links** To revise interpreting a brief, see page 2 of the Revision Guide.

Researching a theme

In finding your own inspiration for visual recording and communication in response to a brief, you can learn from the work of **art and design practitioners** that you research who are relevant to a theme.

1 Identify two art and design works by practitioners in different disciplines, relating to 'Protection'. Explain how you think they connect to the theme.

Work 1: ....

Artist: ....

How they connect to the theme: ....

....

....

....

Work 2: ....

Artist: ....

How they connect to the theme: ....

....

....

....

2 This artwork incorporates visual recording into the final piece. Does the use of broken ceramic plates in the artwork mean that you view the portrait in a different way? Explain your response.

....

....

....

....

....

....

....

....

....

....

....

Julian Schnabel, 1951
Portrait of Dennis Hopper, 1999
Oil, wax, bondo and ceramic plates on wood
© Julian Schnabel / ARS, New York / DACS. Private Collection / Photo © Christie's Images / Bridgeman Images

The artist uses broken ceramic plates, incorporating visual recording into the final piece.

3 Find an innovative artwork or product that incorporates visual recording within the making process, relating to 'Protection'. Explain why you have identified this example as being related to the theme.

> When finding work in your actual assessment, you should include it in your sketchbook or portfolio.

Work 3: ....

Artist: ....

How the artwork incorporates visual recording within the making process: ....

....

....

....

How the artwork connects to the theme: ....

....

....

....

4 Visual recording has changed significantly over time in technique, form and purpose. Give any examples of innovative, traditional and technical styles of visual recording.

> You can use text and images to explain this, or make marks on the images.

....

....

....

....

....

....

....

....

....

....

....

....

....

....

> **Links** To revise researching a theme, see page 3 of the Revision Guide.

Visual recording and communication of content

When researching work by art and design practitioners that are relevant to a theme, you need to understand and explore the way they visually record and communicate in relation to **content**. This involves consideration of theme, ideas, interpretation of a brief and contextual factors.

1 Consider the images on pages 9 and 10 from research relating to 'Protection' and choose the image that relates most closely to your idea of protection. Then analyse the **content** of your chosen image using the questions on page 11.

My chosen image is: ....

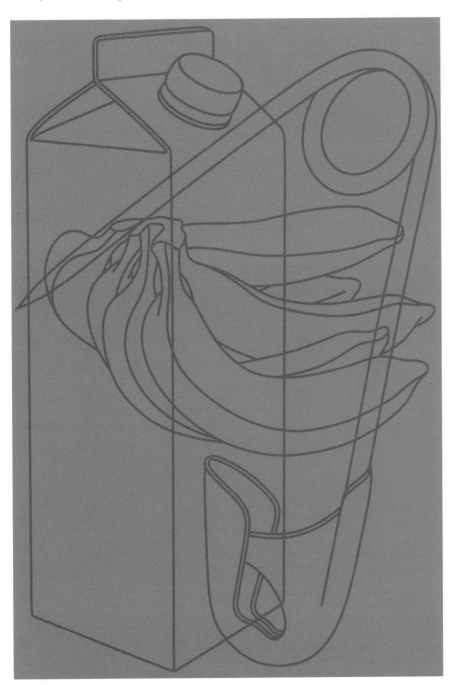

MICHAEL CRAIG-MARTIN *Untitled (magenta/purple)*, 2009 Acrylic on aluminium, 36 x 24 inches, (91.4 x 61cm) CRAIG 2009.0022 GAGOSIAN GALLERY

The Lighthouse of Ostend; Le Phare d'Ostende – Du Vuurtoren van Oostende, 1908
(wash and crayon on paper), Léon Spilliaert (1881–1946).

Use the questions below to help analyse the **content** of your chosen image from pages 9 or 10.

2 Theme: Consider your reading of what the artist may be visually communicating to the audience. How might this relate to a theme of protection? Give a brief explanation of how you have reached this view.

....

....

....

....

....

3 Ideas: Consider the materials the artist has chosen to use. Why might these materials communicate an idea of protection?

....

....

....

....

....

4 Context: Briefly consider how contextual factors relating to protection have changed over time. This will help inform your understanding of how context influences practitioners, and how your own work is influenced.

> Contextual factors can be defined as the impact of other influences on a creative practitioner's work, such as the time or era the work was produced within, or any political, social or cultural influences. You need to investigate how contextual factors influence the work of practitioners and show understanding and application of contextual factors linked to the theme.

....

....

....

....

....

....

....

....

....

....

Links To revise visual recording and communication of content, see page 4 of the Revision Guide.

Understanding and exploring form

It is important to understand and explore the **form** in the work of art and design practitioners as it relates to a theme. To do this you need to explore visual recording and communication in relation to **formal elements**, **use** and **purpose**.

> **Consider:** line, tone, form, texture, colour, pattern, scale, perspective, figure and ground, composition.

1 Research a new work related to 'Protection' or use a work in relation to a theme you have worked with.

My chosen work is: ....

My chosen artist is: ....

2 Use the questions below to analyse form in the work. You don't have to answer all the points as some are more relevant than others, depending on your interest and the artwork. Note your answers around the diagram.

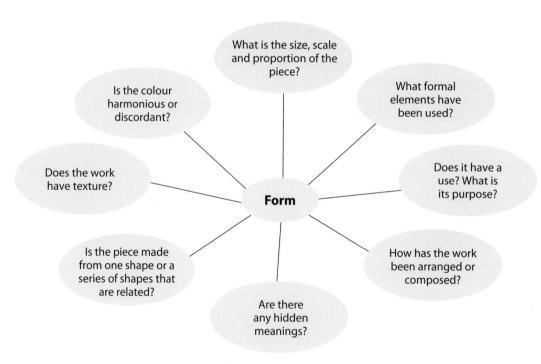

What is the size, scale and proportion of the piece?

What formal elements have been used?

Is the colour harmonious or discordant?

Does it have a use? What is its purpose?

Does the work have texture?

Form

Is the piece made from one shape or a series of shapes that are related?

How has the work been arranged or composed?

Are there any hidden meanings?

> **Links** To revise form in visual recording and communication, see page 5 of the Revision Guide.

Understanding and exploring process

You need to demonstrate an awareness of **process**, considering how materials, techniques and processes are employed by art and design practitioners and how this impacts on your own ideas.

1 Research three images that exemplify your interest in a specific area of the theme 'Protection' or use work in relation to a theme you have worked with. Each image should present a clear connection to each of the following titles.

Image and artist 1: ....

Material/technique/processes: ....

....

Image and artist 2: ....

Material/technique/processes: ....

....

Image and artist 3: ....

Material/technique/processes: ....

....

2 Use the questions below to analyse process in one of the works. You don't have to answer all the points as some are more relevant than others, depending on your interest and the artwork. Note your answers around the diagram.

My chosen work is: ....

What techniques have been used?

What materials have been used?

Has any special equipment been used and how?

Was the work done rapidly or has it been created over a longer period?

Did the artist use sketches, prototypes, maquettes, models?

Process

What were the artist/designer's starting points?

Where was the artwork made?

How, where and why might the work be displayed?

 Links To revise process in visual recording and communication, see page 6 of the Revision Guide.

Understanding and exploring mood

When understanding the ways that others visually record and communicate **mood**, consider the use of **visual language** to convey meaning and creative intentions. You need to identify work by others that generates a similar mood in the audience to the kind you want to communicate.

1 Research a piece of work by an art and design practitioner that uses visual language to create mood in relation to 'Protection' or a theme you have worked with.

My chosen artist and artwork is: ....

2 Use the questions below to identify the key visual language and creative intentions in the work in relation to mood. You don't have to answer all the points as some are more relevant than others, depending on your interest and the artwork. Note your answers around the diagram.

> **Visual language**: scale, size, composition, viewpoint, framing medium, materials, process, production methods, techniques, other elements (use of text, time based, series)

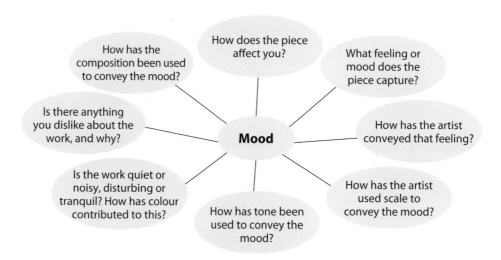

How has the composition been used to convey the mood?

How does the piece affect you?

What feeling or mood does the piece capture?

Is there anything you dislike about the work, and why?

Mood

How has the artist conveyed that feeling?

Is the work quiet or noisy, disturbing or tranquil? How has colour contributed to this?

How has tone been used to convey the mood?

How has the artist used scale to convey the mood?

Guided **3** Consider a piece of your own work where you successfully used visual language to communicate a mood to your audience. Explain your choices and how you physically achieved your intention.

I would describe my work and its intentions as ....

....

I chose colour to impact on the audience by ....

....

When considering texture ....

....

The material I chose to impact on the audience ....

....

> **Links** To revise mood in visual recording and communication, see page 7 of the Revision Guide.

Application and meaning

Meaning is related to the **communication intentions** of the artist or designer. The application of **materials**, **techniques** and **processes** can have a profound impact on the meaning of a work. Understanding how others use them to communicate meaning can impact on considerations for your own work.

1 In the work 'Monument to the Living and the Dead', 2006, Damien Hirst has generated a painting using real butterflies instead of painting them. How does Hirst change the meaning of the canvas by using real butterflies instead of images of butterflies?

....

....

....

....

Guided

2 This is a photo of a handprint on a wall. Explain how the artist has changed the meaning of the handprint.

By placing the handprint on a barrier, the artist has drawn our attention to ....

....

....

Guided

3 Research a piece of work that relates to 'Protection' or use a piece of work you already know, where the practitioner has used the application of materials, techniques and process to impact on communication.

My chosen piece of work is ....

The artist has transformed the meaning by ....

....

....

....

....

> **Links** To revise application and communication of meaning, see page 7 of the Revision Guide.

Understanding and exploring formal elements

Understanding and recording the **formal elements** of the work of practitioners will support your own development. It is important to investigate the work of others through more than just writing. Use all sorts of **visual recording techniques**: the more you try, the more you develop.

> **Consider:** line, tone, form, texture, colour, pattern, scale, perspective, figure and ground, composition.

1 Find a piece of work that relates to each of the formal elements listed in the left hand column. Place an image, or note the work, in the correct place.

> Ways of visually recording from practitioners: copy, trace, draw in different media, draw similar objects, draw from similar source, draw select elements, paint over details, repeat, enlarge, collage, negative, subject focused, repetition, layer, alternative surface.

Guided

2 In the right-hand column, show how you could use a different method to record visually from the work. You could place an image or make a note of what you would do.

Formal elements	Your visual record using different methods
Pattern	Visual record
Line	Visual record
Colour	Visual record
Composition	Visual record

Links To revise formal elements, see page 8 of the Revision Guide.

Visual recording from non-art

You can also visually record from abstract forms of information not normally considered as art and design.

1 Use the internet to find at least two forms of abstract visual data related to 'Protection', or use abstract visual data that you have worked with before relating to a different theme.

> Non-art visual forms might include: maps, signs, tables, charts, diagrams and instructions.

Guided

2 Include the images with an explanation of their relationship to the theme.

Example 1:	The use of graphic lines on a map with a mixed media element, which also makes lines, combines well. I have chosen to include maps as an example of protection as these suggest ways that all nations and people protect themselves. It relates to my focus with the theme as I am looking at the impact of changing boundaries on countries and people, with a focus on immigration.
Example 2:	....
Example 3:	....

 Links To revise recording, see page 9 of the Revision Guide.

Informing your own practice

Most art and design disciplines use visual recording and communication as part of their **development process**. The outcome may not materialise instantly but result from a series of developmental works. For example, an architect will use drawings to record their ideas and record from observations, and a fashion designer might create silhouettes in the production process. Development of your own work can be informed by others.

1 Outline at least **five** methods that artists use to visually record.

....

....

....

....

....

> Many artists talk about their process in interviews.

2 Find an artist or designer that uses visual recording in their development and explain at what stage or stages the visual recording takes place.

....

....

....

....

....

....

Guided **3** Explain how you can inform your own development based on this information.

The reasons I like the way this practitioner uses visual recording are ....

....

....

I will inform my own development in response to this by ....

....

....

....

....

> 🔗 **Links** To revise informing your own practice, see page 9 of the Revision Guide.

Research summary

Consider your research in relation to the brief and **understanding and exploring visual recording and communication** in the work of art and design practitioners through:

- visual recording and communication
- understanding formal elements.

Guided 1 Identify the most important parts of your research so far. If you were taking forward a piece of art and design based on the theme of 'Protection', explain how your research would inform your work.

> Documenting and evaluating your research will be important when considering how to present your research, produce your piece of art or design, and write your commentary.

- When reading and interpreting the brief, my initial response to the

  theme and ideas ....

  ....

  ....

  ....

- My exploration of art and design practitioners, their ideas and imagery ....

  ....

  ....

  ....

  ....

- It was interesting to investigate and understand how contextual factors link to a theme ....

  ....

  ....

  ....

  ....

- The types of visual recording I find most relevant are ....

  ....

  ....

  ....

  ....

- Research into materials, techniques and processes led me to consider ....

  ....

  ....

  ....

  ....

- The way practitioners use visual language to present a mood that I find most relevant is ....

....

....

....

....

- The formal elements in others' work that appear the most useful to my approach to the theme

'Protection' are ....

....

....

....

....

- Non-art helped me record interesting visual forms ....

....

....

....

....

- When examining how the use of visual recording and communication informs and is applied to my

own work ....

....

....

....

....

- The directions in which I would take a piece of art and design relating to the theme 'Protection'

are ....

....

....

....

....

....

....

Links To revise using visual recording and communication skills, see page 10 of the Revision Guide.

Recording from primary sources

Observational recording from **primary sources** is critical to your development process, presentation of your research and final piece of art and design. Looking at things **purposefully** and **investigating them visually** can provide a rich space for ideas generation and understanding.

> Look at the latest Sample Assessment Material on the Pearson website for information on what is required for inclusion of primary sources in the development and presentation of your work.

> Use the questions below to ensure you are clear on the value of recording from primary sources and what they can offer.

Guided 1 Explain what recording from primary sources involves.

Recording from primary sources involves looking at real objects, places and forms to observe

them directly in order to record them. For example, ...

....

Mark making can also ....

....

Guided 2 Outline some key advantages of recording from primary sources.

Accessing primary sources provides opportunity to observe and record from different angles.

For example, ...

....

Selecting and positioning what to record is interesting because ....

....

Choosing to focus on the whole object or on details can ....

....

Primary sources give first-hand experience, and as individuals see things differently each

recording will be a unique interpretation, so ....

....

3 Make a list of primary sources that you could use to explore and generate ideas in relation to 'Protection'.

> These should be realistic and achievable. Thinking cleverly about your primary sources can provide creative solutions.

Primary source	How it can be accessed
1	
2	
3	
4	

Links To revise 2D recording from primary sources, see pages 11–12 of the Revision Guide.

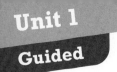
2D primary recording

Primary sources contain a variety of **forms**, **textures**, **colours** and **shapes** that can be recorded in **2D** using, for example, **illustrations**, **print** or **textiles**. Consider a wide range of 2D mark-making techniques such as single line and multiple lines (e.g. rotate, clone, rip, cut), tone (e.g. blend, wash, cross-hatch, stipple), texture (e.g. layer, media, focus, dodge), form (e.g. silhouette, perspective), colour (e.g. paint, pastels, collage) and scale.

⟩ **Guided** ⟩   **1** Create an observational recording from a primary source related to 'Protection', or use observational recordings from primary sources that you have already completed for an existing work.

> You could take a picture of a drawing in a sketchbook and place it here.

Continuous line

2 Record from a primary source using at least **two** different media, or demonstrate your skills in doing this from work already completed.

Media 1	Media 2

3 Explain your choice of primary sources, the methods you explored and ideas generated by the work.

....

....

....

....

....

....

🔗 **Links** To revise 2D primary recording, see pages 12 and 14 of the Revision Guide.

Secondary sources and 2D recording

Your work should build creatively on a combination of primary and secondary recording. **Visual recording** from **secondary sources** involves exploring the **internet**, **books**, **magazines**, **journals**, **film**, **photographs**, **animation**, **video**, **music** and **audio**.

Guided

1 Select an image from a secondary source that links with the theme of 'Protection'. Use one of the listed methods in each box to visually record it in 2D. Use a method not listed for the last recording. You could instead use visual recording that you have already completed from secondary sources for an existing work.

> Show your use of different media as well as methods. It is important you are selective in your choice of media: it should have a logical relationship to your interest in the theme. While there is no right and wrong, you should make conscious decisions that you can justify. You could take a picture of your visual recordings and place them below.

trace outline, observational study, draw a detail	combine collage and drawing, copy in paint, trace and repeat, charcoal
contour drawing, continuous line, negative space, silhouette	My fourth method is ....

2 For each method, explain the reason behind your use of media and its relationship to the theme. Did your choices work? How were the characteristics of your source reflected by the method and medium?

....

....

....

....

....

....

....

....

Links To revise secondary sources and 2D recording, see pages 11 and 15 of the Revision Guide.

Primary and secondary 3D recording

Different specialisms in art and design require **3D recording and communication**. Sometimes this is a technical requirement, for others it suits the planning and development of a project or an artist's or designer's methods. Consider options such as carving, cutting, shaping, forming, joining and sculpting.

Guided 1 Outline three different practices that would use 3D recording or communication.

Practice 1: Animators might make a rough model of a character to ....

....

....

....

Practice 2: ....

....

....

....

Practice 3: ....

....

....

....

2 Create one 3D recording from a primary or secondary source in relation to 'Protection', or describe what you would create. You could use a 3D recording that you have already created in relation to a different theme. Explain how it helps develop your work in relation to a theme.

> You could photograph your idea and place it below. You may want to record your idea from different angles.

Image:

Explanation: ....

....

....

....

....

Links To revise 3D recording, see pages 11 and 13 of the Revision Guide.

Camera recording with purpose

It is important to appreciate the difference between recording with a camera and using mark-making methods. When using a camera or video, use it **creatively** and make the most of its unique properties to maximise the **impact** your pictures have on the outcome. Recording with a lens can **combine** with other methods of recording and analysis of results can create a fuller picture.

Guided 1 Explain how you can use a camera or video to record with purpose in three different ways.

Method 1: I would make sure I focus the camera on specific details rather than getting quick

general shots because ....

....

Method 2: ....

....

....

Method 3: ....

....

....

Guided 2 Use a camera to record a relevant object or scene related to 'Protection' or choose an example you have already worked with in relation to a theme and record the results below.

	I have used the camera here as a means to record different textures that I think could make interesting armour for the theme 'Protection'. I plan to make a computer game character and wanted to have futuristic armour that didn't have the texture of traditional armour. This gives me a way of comparing them. These were objects I found around the house, but that could transform well.
My example	

3 Explain how your process of recording supports your research and exploration.

....

....

....

....

Links To revise image recording with camera and video, see page 14 of the Revision Guide.

Recording through manipulation

Consider how you can **manipulate** images to present details or viewpoints that might otherwise be missed.

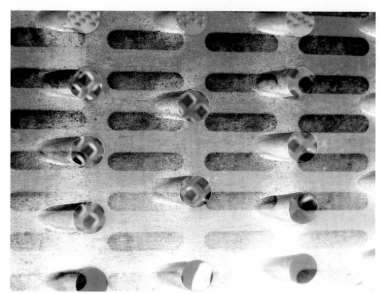

> The process of manipulation can be quite experimental.

This artist has blended together the images of armour-textured shots from a kitchen (see page 25) as a means of visual recording.

1 Manipulate one of your images that relate to 'Protection' or another theme in at least **two** ways from the following list:

- brightness and contrast
- levels/curves
- filters
- image trace

- layer
- blend
- cut-out
- saturation

- juxtaposition
- materials-based manipulation, e.g. scratching, distorting, overpainting, photocopying, bleaching

> You can use simple programs or applications to achieve many of these effects digitally. Alternatively, use methods like double exposure, superposition, framing and composition, and explore the physical characteristics of your camera. Non-digital manipulation, such as materials-based manipulation, is also effective.

Method 1	Method 2

 Links To revise manipulating images, see page 14 of the Revision Guide.

Recording summary

Consider your work in **developing visual recording and communication skills**. Evaluate the quality and breadth of your visual recording including observational recordings from primary sources and visual recordings using secondary sources. Documenting and evaluating this work will be important when considering how to present your research, deciding the direction of your final piece of work and communicating the theme in different ways, for example through style, medium, technique, interpretation. It will also support your commentary.

Guided

1 Select two of the best pieces you have recorded in relation to 'Protection' or another theme you have worked with. When evaluating which work to select, refer to the brief (page 2) to be clear your work shows what is required.

> You can scan or print pages or images if you need to.

Piece 1: observational recording from primary sources	Piece 2: visual recording from secondary sources

Guided

2 Explain why you chose the pieces and evaluate your recordings in a critical way. Did you succeed, fail or discover an unexpected result?

<u>Piece 1</u>

- This recording provides insight into ....
....
....
....

- The process was appropriate because ....
....
....
....

- This recording shows the influence of the work of ....
....
....
....

- Contextual factors of the recording link to the theme through ....
....
....
....

<u>Piece 2</u>

- This recording provides insight into ....
....
....
....

- The process was appropriate because ....
....
....
....

- This recording shows the influence of the work of ....
....
....
....

- Contextual factors of the recording link to the theme through ....
....
....
....

<u>Pieces 1 and 2</u>

- I have explored a variety of different recordings, including ....
....
....
....
....

- I could develop these recordings into a piece of art or design ....
....
....
....
....

2D and 3D ideas generation

When you have used your visual recording and communication skills to record from primary and secondary sources in relation to a theme, you move on to **develop and extend** your skills and ideas through **experimentation and investigation**. Start by considering **2D and 3D ideas generation**.

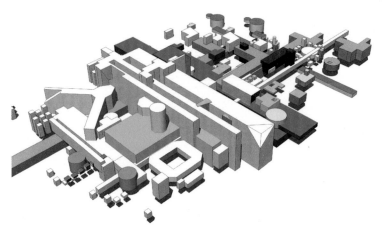

> **2D ideas generation:** mind maps, word association, designing, drawing, sketching, working from primary and secondary sources, photography, screen-based design work
>
> **3D ideas generation:** drawing in 3D, samples, models, maquettes, test pieces, 3D software

3D drawing in SketchUp is an effective way of generating ideas for forms.

1 Use 2D or 3D techniques to visualise an idea of a piece you would like to create for the theme 'Protection'. You could briefly sketch ideas by hand or on computer or briefly describe your techniques and ideas. You could instead use work that you have already produced in relation to a different theme.

Guided

2 Explain which of your previous sources have inspired these ideas.

I found it an interesting idea to combine the working process and the visual records of ....

....

....

....

....

....

....

Links To revise 2D and 3D ideas generation, see pages 18–19 of the Revision Guide.

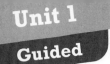
Experimenting to visually record

To **extend** your visual recording, consider how you can investigate and experiment with **different and diverse materials**, **techniques** and **processes**.

1 Visualise your idea or elements of your idea for 'Protection' using two different surfaces. You could briefly create or describe your idea. You could instead use work that you have already produced in relation to a different theme. Include reasons for your choices.

> For example, you could consider using wallpaper, card, coloured paper, maps, photographs, pages from books, envelopes, fabric, textured paper, newspaper, magazines or other kinds of found surfaces like wood.

I tried drawing directly onto the pages of a book about protection and my theme. I liked the way the words came through by chance and added to the drawing.

Surface 1	Surface 2

....

....

....

....

2 Visualise your idea or elements of your idea for 'Protection' using two different and diverse media. You could briefly create or describe your idea. You could instead use work that you have already produced in relation to a different theme. Include reasons for your choices.

Media 1	Media 2

....

....

....

....

3 Visualise your idea or elements of your idea for 'Protection' using a technical drawing method relevant to your specialism. You could briefly create or describe your idea. You could instead use work that you have already produced in relation to a different theme. Include reasons for your choices.

Choose from: perspective, isometric, exploded, plan, oblique, axonometric, orthographic, gestural, fashion illustration, subtractive, CAD, cutaway, wireframe, cel, storyboard, calligraphy, print, etch, engraving, layout.

Technical drawing method

....

....

....

....

Links To revise investigating diverse recording materials, see page 20 of the Revision Guide.

Manipulating for creative intentions

To **extend** your visual recording and communication, **explore** how manipulating the materials, techniques and processes you use changes the way your work communicates your **creative intentions**.

1   Explain what you would like to communicate about a theme and then connect the materials, techniques and processes to your communication intention. This could be in relation to 'Protection' or any theme you have worked with.

> For example: *I aim to communicate the idea of protection through defence and the use of weapons such as nuclear missiles in modern warfare. I would explore ways of manipulating linear work for my outcome including clean digital lines to reference the lines of defence, angular shapes like the gridlines on maps used to pinpoint targets and graphic blocks of colour evoking grids seen in weapons control rooms.*

....

....

....

....

....

....

2   Communicate your idea on a theme using manipulation of different materials, techniques and processes. You could briefly create or describe your idea. Include reasons for your choices.

Materials	Techniques	Processes

....

....

....

....

....

....

Links   To revise manipulating materials for creative intentions, see page 21 of the Revision Guide.

Development summary

Consider your work in **extending your own visual recording and communication skills** through experimentation and investigation. Documenting and evaluating this work will be important when considering how to present your research and when making choices for your final piece of art and design. It will also support your commentary.

1 Use clear and focused bullet points to explain the key things you developed while working on your ideas.

> You could consider how your images and materials changed and the reason why. For example:
> - *Materials testing – I needed a medium for sculpting that was both see-through and easy to mould…*

2D and 3D ideas generation (see page 29)

....

....

....

....

....

....

....

Experimenting with diverse materials, techniques and processes (see page 30)

....

....

....

....

....

....

....

Exploration through manipulating materials, techniques and processes (see page 32)

....

....

....

....

....

....

....

Considering presentation of research

The way you **select and present** evidence of your **visual recording and research** is very important. There are many factors to reflect on in advance, prior to mounting. Make a plan that considers what you will be assessed on and space available. You can then determine the content to include and ways of presenting it.

> For details of research presentation in your actual assessment, such as the size and number of presentation sheets, ask your tutor or look at the latest Sample Assessment Material on the Pearson website. For example, you might have to mount your work onto a given number of A2 presentation sheets.
>
> Pay attention to what you will be assessed on in your actual assessment which might include, for example:
> · the quality of your research into art and design practitioners
> · the quality and breadth of your visual recording and research
> · your understanding and application of contextual factors linked to a theme.

Guided

1 Identify the most important aspects of research to present, and consider the pros and cons of different possible methods. Look back at the summaries of research (pages 19–20), recording (pages 27–28) and development (page 33) to guide selection criteria and methods of presentation.

Method 1: I could photograph my work and sketchbook pages and use Photoshop to organise

the information. The benefits of doing this would be ....

....

....

Method 2: ....

....

....

Method 3: ....

....

....

Guided

2 Consider how you might focus your presentation if using three A2 presentation sheets.

> Think about how you will show the development of your ideas. Show a clear narrative of the progression of your work.

Sheet 1: I could show ....

The benefits of doing this would be ....

....

Sheet 2: I could show ....

The benefits of doing this would be ....

....

Sheet 3: I could show ....

The benefits of doing this would be ....

....

3 Consider different layouts you might use to present your material. Think about the audience and the level of consistency throughout the presentation. Here are some examples.

Title					
	Image	Image	Image	Image	Image
	Text	Text	Text	Text	Text

1 Early starting point, sketches and draft ideas.

2 Models and maquettes made from sketches.

3 Final outcome.

> You could consider using narrative or sequence to show your development and exploration of the theme on individual pages.
>
> Methods could include annotated diagrams that link images together in a sequence. You may want to use arrows or numbers to indicate the sequence.

4 If using three A2 boards for your development, sketch here how you might present your work, prior to showing your final outcome. Refer to the notes you created on the previous page.

Research presentation 1	Research presentation 2	Research presentation 3

Links To revise deciding on an idea, recording the development process, annotating your work and producing work, see pages 22–24 and pages 28–31 of the Revision Guide.

Producing art or design

Consider how you would use your research, recording and development to **produce one fully developed piece of art or design** that responds to the theme and **visually communicates** your idea about 'Protection' or another theme you have worked with.

> Your final piece would reflect your research and preparatory work, to demonstrate:
> - your response to the theme
> - your use of materials, techniques and processes
> - your ability to communicate your creative intentions.
>
> You will not need to actually produce this piece of art and design for this Revision Workbook.
>
> For your actual assessment, ask your tutor or check the Sample Assessment Material on the Pearson website for details relating to whether the piece can be an **extension and development** of work produced during the research and recording stage or a **stand-alone piece of work** informed by the research and development.
>
> Pay attention also to what you will be assessed on. Consider, for example: your interpretation and communication of the theme and your ability to manipulate materials, techniques and processes to communicate your creative intentions.

1 Outline a fully developed piece of art and design that you would propose. Explain your reasons in relation to the work you have completed and how you will demonstrate the points listed above.

> Reflect on your work in the research and preparatory stage. Look back especially to the brief (pages 2–5), and the summaries of research (pages 19–20), recording (pages 27–28) and development (page 33).

....

....

....

....

....

....

....

....

....

....

....

....

....

....

....

....

2 Use these questions to make notes that help refine your ideas.

(a) Use of imagery – does it communicate what you expect it to?

....

....

(b) Contextual factors – how have these been considered?

....

....

(c) Manipulation of materials, techniques and processes – are you using the most appropriate methods to interpret and communicate your response to the theme and creative intentions?

....

....

3 Briefly describe or sketch your idea visually in 2D or 3D. Use annotations to explain how it is part of the production process and any refinement process used through testing out and evaluation.

My idea for a fully developed piece of art and design

Guided

4 Explain how your choices have affected, or been affected by, the process and the outcome.

I would use this technique because ....

....

....

I would use this process to make the work because ....

....

....

I would use this material because ....

....

....

> Tools and equipment are also important choices you have to make that are part of your process.

Links To revise appropriate methods, refining ideas and your own work, and creating an outcome, see pages 25–27 of the Revision Guide.

Applying skills for creative intentions

When applying visual recording skills to **communicate creative intention**s, you need to be able to explain what your piece communicates and how it does this.

Guided **1** How does your work communicate your creative intentions?

The artwork relates to the audience because ....

....

....

....

The aspects of contemporary visual language it uses are ....

> Consider imagery, context and manipulation of materials.

....

....

....

....

....

Guided **2** Show how you could apply your work to at least **two** products, using the spaces on page 39. You could describe or sketch your ideas. For example, you could frame your piece and its message in a commercial context. Explain your reasons for selecting these products in relation to 'Protection' or a theme you have worked with.

> For example, you could put a print on a plate or a visual on a website.

Example:

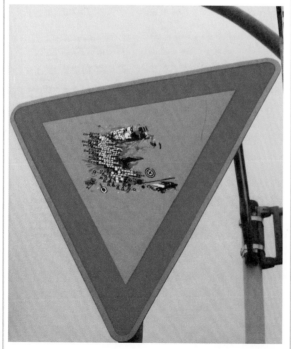

I have considered applying my product to street signage that I have photographed as a means of protecting the public. With my new image design, I would adjust from typical signage that uses bold red lines and blank spaces. My new signage uses experimental graphics, typography and colour textures. Normally signage represents things visually, but mine tries to reflect the smells of public transport, arranged in a way that they look like they are smells rising from something.

I just think that life is a bit more complicated than simple icons and I wanted to explore the idea of more subtle signage as a means of protecting people.

Example 1 of applying my work to product

Example 2 of applying my work to product

Considering presentation factors

The way you present evidence of your fully developed piece of art or design is very important. There are many factors to reflect on in advance, prior to mounting and submission.

Guided 1 Describe how you could demonstrate elements of your work through your visual presentation.

> Use the prompts to help you structure your answer.

I can demonstrate the texture or finish of the work by taking a close-up picture that shows a detail. For the shiny bits I could try to reflect it into the light. Another alternative would be to include a swatch of the material on the presentation sheet itself.

I can demonstrate the small details of the work by ....

....

....

I can clarify the materials used in the work by ....

....

....

I can clarify the process used in the creative process by ....

....

....

For time-based work, I could clarify the length by ....

....

....

Guided 2 Reflect on how the audience for your work or product can impact on the presentation on the sheets.

My audience would include ....

Similar work is presented or packaged in styles like ....

....

....

The visual language for this audience needs to be ....

....

....

The written language needs to be ....

....

....

3 Reflect on how each of the following examples has used the space for the presentation of the fully developed piece of art and design.

| Example 1 | Example 2 | Example 3 |

Example 1: Alzheimer's — Mark-making that shows the destructive power of memory loss.

Example 2: THE NEED FOR A GOOD DIET.

Example 3: An advertising campaign generating awareness of genetic modification of human genes to be placed in doctors' surgeries.
Baby in a bottle
12cm x 4cm tube
Acetate line image
Rolled paper text

Questions	Example 1	Example 2	Example 3
Which of the three has the least text information on the scale and materials?			
Which clarifies the scale, media and technical information the most?			
Which has the least information, visual or text, about the scale and media of the outcome?			
Which of the three may confuse the viewer as to the outcome?			
Which of the three seems to include development work?			

4 Compare and contrast the three outcomes and choose the work that you think best communicates to the audience. Explain why and justify your reasons.

....

....

....

....

....

....

....

....

....

....

Links To revise planning your research presentation, see pages 28–31 of the Revision Guide.

Considering presentation of final piece

You will need to practise making the presentation of your fully developed piece of art or design. You can do this digitally or physically and you need to demonstrate:

- your response to the theme – consider your interpretation and communication of the theme
- your ability to manipulate materials, techniques and processes to communicate your creative intentions.

1   Outline **three** ways you could draw attention to how you have addressed each of the above points.

....

....

....

....

....

....

2   Evaluate the most effective ways of presenting the outcome you have planned for 'Protection' or another theme you have worked with, using physical or digital media. Consider what you will include and the layout you might use, for example:

- large images of the outcome on its own
- all the images being taken from different angles
- a combination of an image of the work on its own and images showing details and development
- a combination of an image of the work on its own and images of the work being used in a functional setting.

> For your actual assessment, ask your tutor or check the up-to-date Sample Assessment Material on the Pearson website for details on the presentation of your image. Pay attention to information in relation to:
> - any number or size restrictions
> - the images being of sufficient size to show the quality of the work
> - work that is intended to be accessed digitally to be on PDF documents
> - 3D and larger pieces being photographed and an indication of scale
> - a maximum of four photographs showing the final 3D piece (one image of the work in its entirety and three further images of different angles and/or details).
>
> The details of assessment may change, so always make sure you are up to date.

Presenting my developed piece of art or design

 Links   To revise planning your research presentation, see pages 28–31 of the Revision Guide.

Commentary on research

You will need to **write a commentary** to accompany your presentations, so make sure you document your research and exploration of materials and methods used. Show your ability to evaluate outcomes in a way that connects your research with your creative intentions and identifies development needs and strengths and weaknesses in your own work.

1 Outline how you used visual recording in primary and secondary research.

I have visually recorded from primary research by: ....

....

I have visually recorded from secondary research by: ....

....

I have connected the media and techniques used to record to the project theme by: ....

....

I have used the recordings to generate ideas by: ....

....

2 Read this extract from a commentary about primary and secondary research. Note at least **four** things that could be improved.

> I like working from my imagination so I wasn't focused on the research side too much. I liked looking at military stuff and the camouflage they use for protection. I took lots of photos as drawing from these wasn't really necessary. I just stuck to the American camouflage as it looked the most visually appealing and I found this online in Google Images so it wasn't necessary to do much primary research.

(a) ....

(b) ....

(c) ....

(d) ....

3 Compare the first extract to the following one and make notes on ways this is an improvement.

> Many of the artists relevant to the project had made observations from similar sources. While primary sources were difficult to access, it made sense to think differently about camouflage, and not just as a military tool, so I recorded how camouflage is used across a range of natural and man-made environments. Working with a range of media and processes to visually record, I was able to analyse which camouflage worked and this provoked questions about the need for protection in our society.

(a) ....

(b) ....

(c) ....

(d) ....

> **Links** To revise the written commentary, see page 37 of the Revision Guide.

Commentary on ideas generation

Commenting on the ideas generation stage of your project is important. One reason is that it clarifies whether you know strategies for developing ideas.

1 Note **two** other reasons why commenting on the ideas generation stage of your project is important.

....

....

2 Describe **three** ideas generation processes you used for exploring visual communication.

> Did you use methods from other artists and designers?

(a) ....

(b) ....

(c) ....

> **Guided**

3 Complete the following statements about how you generated your ideas for 'Protection' or any other theme you have worked with.

I explored a range of ideas before ....

It made sense to use two ideas generation methods like ....

....

I used these methods because ....

....

The most traditional method of ideas generation was ....

The most unusual method of ideas generation was ....

Comparing the benefits of carrying out the ideas generation process with not carrying it out,

my visual recording would ....

....

....

....

....

My work would communicate ....

....

....

....

....

....

> **Links** To revise reviewing ideas generation, see page 32 of the Revision Guide.

Commentary on formal elements

When writing about the physical object you have created, remember that others will have no idea of its purpose or intentions. Your commentary is your chance to show your audience how successfully elements have come together in your work. Complete the table below in relation to the theme 'Protection' or any theme you have worked with.

1 Note some formal elements and imagery chosen for your piece that you can comment on.

> If there isn't space to discuss all the formal elements or imagery, focus on the most important ones.

	Formal elements and imagery
1	
2	
3	
4	
5	

2 Describe why the three most important formal elements from question 1 were chosen for your work.

....

....

....

....

....

3 Compare the extracts from two learner commentaries about formal elements within art and design work.

Extract 1: The most interesting aspect about the theme of protection for me was to emphasise our vulnerability. When I think about it, the use of strong, bold materials is connected to it. I chose to use a monochrome palette with clear structure to emphasise the strength provided by the work and the sense of protection it can give. The composition is balanced so that the aggressive element takes the largest portion of the work, but the subject and individual within the image is very small to suggest their vulnerability. The artists I have looked at do this in interesting ways and I thought it would be good to use the same composition.

Extract 2: I worked on this piece for a long time because I needed it to look visually interesting. My work is about the beauty protective clothing has and I tried to make something beautiful. Life isn't all about the ordinary. People need to see beauty in everything to make them happy whatever they are experiencing. For me, bright and pretty things can give hope regardless of the situation people feel they are in. I haven't seen anything like this before so wanted to create something new.

Analysis of extracts	Extract 1	Extract 2
Which relates the theme to the formal elements used?		
Which doesn't connect the formal elements to the communication intentions?		
Which objectively discusses the communication intentions?		
Which makes bold statements about the audience's needs?		
Which suggests learning from others?		

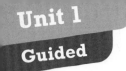

Commentary on Ms, Ts and Ps

Your commentary needs to evaluate how well the materials, techniques and processes you chose worked in the final outcome and during the development process.

1 Read the following extracts from commentaries then state which extract(s) best fit the aspect of analysis.

Extracts from learner commentaries

A I had this fantastic idea from the outset to use shiny materials like armour to emphasise protection. Everyone always connects strength with hard and new materials. My outcomes use shiny fabric because it is beautiful to look at. It was just incredibly powerful to look at all these solid metals on a garment. Metal is strong and everyone will recognise what I am trying to communicate.

B I wasn't sure about the idea to start with, but wanted to understand what it meant to be vulnerable before I addressed the theme. This led me to investigating vulnerable groups within our society and how they experience and voice their concerns about the vulnerable in our society. It became clear that the oppressors used wealth as a way to have power over the vulnerable, which is why I picked the material of money within my work. It seemed interesting that such a basic material can have such an impact on society. Everyone will recognise the use of money as a material and be able to relate to it.

C I worked really hard on this project, more than any other I have done. I wanted to get better at this technique and knew I had to develop it for university. Within computer games animation, it is really important to be able to draw from real life. People in a life drawing situation always look vulnerable and in need of protection so showing them in difficult positions was going to be the perfect scenario.

D Life drawings always looked vulnerable. Seeing people exposed in this way triggered an idea to use this as part of my project. I had seen artists use the body to present the idea of protection so I tried adding my own collages of these to life drawings I had created. This led to taking pictures of people wearing objects and costumes that I could then use as a basis for my work in costume. I wanted to create a pattern that felt invincible so I used the strongest photos I took as a basis for the outcome. The ideas generation was really useful and helped me develop varied shapes I had not seen before. From these, I was able to make toiles and then a final garment that was soft, but looked very protective.

Analysis of extracts	Extract
Which extract contextualises the use of materials most?	
Which makes assumptions about the audience, rather than giving a balanced point of view?	
Which extract focuses most on the future instead of the project?	
Which relates the process of production most to the communication intentions?	
Which relates most to relevant principles for the unit?	
Which discusses process as a valid principle for creating the product?	

> Guided > 2 How did the materials, techniques and processes you chose relate to 'Protection' or your chosen theme?

The materials I chose relate to the theme because ....

....

The techniques I chose relate to the theme because ....

....

The processes I chose related to the theme because ....

....

Links To revise sources, methods and materials, see page 38 of the Revision Guide.

Commentary on creative decisions

Your commentary should reflect on the most significant of your refinements and creative decisions. Balance the ones that you were forced to make with ones where you were able to make informed, directed and creative choices.

You can't discuss all your refinements and creative decisions – choose the ones that had the most impact.

1 Tick the statements below that support your commentary on refinement and creative decisions.

Statement	Tick
Artists and designers make decisions based on instinct alone.	
Artists and designers make creative decisions based on what they are trying to communicate.	
Artists and designers want to make beautiful things and this is the guiding principle.	
Some solutions to creative problems come through trial and error.	
Artists and designers should be free to use materials, techniques and processes however they want.	
Artists and designers use evaluation to work through a process of improvement.	
Artists and designers can learn about the appropriateness of materials, techniques and processes used by others.	
All observation should focus on what other artists and designers have done.	

2 Write your own commentary about your refinement and creative decisions on the theme of 'Protection' or any theme you have worked with. Include:

- the audience
- mistakes you made
- two major decisions
- a period of testing and evaluation
- an area of art, design or culture you used to inform your decisions
- what your aim was
- an alternative approach you considered.

Your creative process goes through stages. Every time you try or test a material, technique or process of making it is an opportunity to change direction. Your decisions are made in order to produce a better outcome.

....

....

....

....

....

....

....

....

....

Links To revise creative decisions and refinements, see pages 33–36 of the Revision Guide.

3 Assess the following extract from a commentary.

Extract from learner commentary

As I'm interested in product design, I tried to find a commercial product I could apply my work to. As I am lucky enough to have chickens in my garden, the theme of protection was used to create packaging to sell the eggs. The more visual recording I undertook of the eggs and how they are represented historically in nursery rhymes such as 'Humpty Dumpty', the more I felt they got a bad reputation as symbolising fragility. When undertaking research into eggs, it was clear that they are one of nature's wonders when it comes to strength and the shape they are formed in is incredibly efficient at protecting the vulnerable interior. In fact, I found that the arch shape has been used structurally in engineering terms since at least the Romans.

I moved on to trying to visually record egg shapes, colours and textures in as many ways as I could, such as: dropping them onto paper from a height, scanning the actual shells, traditional painting on eggs, and covering them in ink and rolling them across paper. This gave me a wealth of images, but didn't visually present their inherent strength and I was worried the consumer would just find pretty packaging, but wouldn't understand what I was trying to communicate. I realised there may have been some missing research, so I investigated how strong eggs actually are by finding simple science experiments online in the Scientific American. Just doing these experiments provided a really interesting set of visual and practical experiments that were so much fun to do. People don't seem to like packaging that doesn't offer them anything – that's why there are cartoons on cereal boxes – so it made sense to just translate the details of the egg strength experiment onto the packaging.

Once I had this information, I was able to use lots of different illustration techniques based on my photos of the experimentation. I used a conventional egg box and put different labels on and compared and contrasted these. For it to stand out on the shelf, I needed there to be a bold contrast with most supermarket egg boxes that seem to have colours taken from chickens themselves or farmland.

(a) Why did the learner move away from their initial visual recording?

....

....

(b) What are the most significant points of decision making and how are these framed?

....

....

(c) Why has the learner referenced other products, and discussed the consumer?

....

....

(d) How was testing used to help make creative decisions?

....

....

(e) How might the learner have discovered 'people don't seem to like packaging that doesn't offer them anything'? Describe two different ways the writer might have researched this issue.

....

....

Commentary on purpose, meaning and intent

Your commentary needs to demonstrate your ability to analyse the use of visual language and formal elements in your own and others' work and show quality and detail in your explanations and justifications for decisions.

1 Explain **three** key pieces of information that contributed to your intentions for the work on the theme of 'Protection' or any other theme you have worked with.

> Art and design can have a range of purposes, for example practical, psychological or experiential. Not everyone will receive your work in the same way or understand it perfectly but you can do practical things to aim for this.

....

....

....

2 Explain how your work relates to the chosen theme by including information on:

- the materials
- the techniques
- the processes of production
- the formal elements
- the meaning.

....

....

....

....

....

Guided ▷ **3** Identify **one** positive and **one** negative aspect of what your work communicates and give a reason for your judgement.

> It is important to move beyond personal judgements – frame your evaluation within practical reasons.

One strength with what it communicates is:

....

....

....

....

The reason I think this is because:

....

....

....

....

An issue with what the work communicates is:

....

....

....

....

The reason I think this is because:

....

....

....

....

Links To revise commenting on communication, see page 39 of the Revision Guide.

Writing a focused commentary

Guided > **1** List **six** key aspects of your creative process to focus on. Rank them in the order you will write about them.

1	My starting point – using primary and secondary visual research	2	....
	....		....
	....		....

Guided > **2** Explain how you can find solutions to the issues below to help write a strong commentary.

Issue: Being overly subjective and using personal opinions Solution:	Issue: Assuming the reader knows me and my project Solution: ....
Issue: Not covering all of the important points Solution:	Issue: Repetition and overuse of specific words Solution: ....
Issue: Not having an ending Solution:	Issue: Saying everything is perfect Solution: ....

3 Rewrite the following learner commentary to cover the same points but within 80 words.

> Write concisely and be specific and precise.

I found I had too many ideas and it was difficult to decide which way to go. I tried looking at artists who create work relating to my theme and to include non-art related research to enhance my portfolio. I have learned how to explore new subjects and gain the greatest amount of potential out of them through intensive artist research and exploration of different media, materials and techniques. My skills and knowledge have broadened and intensified since starting on the project. I have learned to follow ideas until a product or result is achieved and then move on and explore new ideas. I have also learned graphic methods of metaphor and representation that support the visualisation of my ideas into objects and products.

....

....

....

....

....

....

....

Revision activities

Although the revision task refers to completion and mounting of pieces of art and design for revision activities 1 and 2 and a written commentary for revision activity 3, this Workbook will only require you to focus on the associated skills within a practical revision timeframe. You may not actually have created your own piece of art and design in response to the theme of 'Protection'. When responding to the following activities, you can refer to an imagined piece of art and design, or to a piece of art and design that you have already created in response to a different theme.

Ask your tutor or check the latest Sample Assessment Material on the Pearson website to establish what is required in your actual assessment and how many hours you have for your assessed activities so that you can complete them within the allocated time. Pay attention to any details such as whether there is a word limit for your commentary.

Revision activity 1

Consider how you would **select** and **mount** work from your research and preparatory stage that demonstrates:
- your ability to visually communicate a theme in different ways
- your exploration of ideas, imagery and visual language
- your exploration of materials and methods of recording
- at least one observational recording from a primary source
- your research into art and design practitioners
- contextual factors you have investigated.

Make sure you show:
- the **quality** of your research into art and design practitioners
- the **quality and breadth** of your visual recording and research
- your **understanding and application** of contextual factors linked to a theme.

For your actual assessment, pay attention to the size and number of presentation sheets allowed and whether your research and preparatory work should be mounted onto no more than three A2 sheets.

 Look back at your work on pages 34–35. Outline a final selection of work that you would mount and the layout you would use. Note how the work demonstrates the above criteria.

Presentation sheet 1	Presentation sheet 2	Presentation sheet 3

Be aware of how you can use key words and phrases in your commentary in Revision activity 3 on page 53.

Revision activity 2

Consider how you would mount the work/images of your fully developed piece of art or design.

The work produced should demonstrate:

- your response to a theme
- your use of materials, techniques and processes
- your ability to communicate your creative intentions.

Make sure you show:

- your interpretation and communication of a theme
- your ability to **manipulate** materials, techniques and processes to communicate your creative intentions.

In your actual assessment, pay attention to the size and number of presentation sheets allowed and whether your fully developed piece of art or design should be mounted onto one sheet of A2 paper. Notice whether this can be an extension and development of work produced during the research and recording stage or a stand-alone piece of work informed by the research and development.

 Look back at your work on pages 40–42. Outline a final choice of work that you would mount and the layout you would use. Annotate or make notes to show how your work would meet the points outlined above.

Developed piece of art/design

 Links Be aware of how you can use key words and phrases in your commentary in Revision activity 3 on page 53.

Revision activity 3

Consider how you would produce a written commentary to accompany the presentation of your work for Revision activity 1 and Revision activity 2. This should include explanations on:

- your interpretation of a theme
- the art and design practitioners you researched and how they influenced your work
- the primary and secondary sources you used in response to a theme
- the visual recording methods and material you used
- your own visual recording and communication in relation to a theme, including key decisions made, strengths and weaknesses and areas for improvement in your own work.

Make sure you show:

- your **analysis** of the use of visual language and formal elements in your own and others' work
- the **quality and detail** in your explanations and justifications for decisions made.

> Use your work from pages 43–50 to write an outline plan of key points you would include in your commentary that would demonstrate the above criteria. You could use a flow diagram to show your outline plan visually.

....

....

....

....

....

....

....

....

....

....

....

....

....

....

....

....

....

....

....

....

....

Unit 2: Critical and Contextual Studies in Art and Design

Your set task

Unit 2 will be assessed through a task, which will be set by Pearson. You will need to use your understanding of contextual research and visual analysis to critically analyse the work of art and design practitioners and improve your own practice as you carry out research and prepare a response to a provided brief.

Your Revision Workbook

This Workbook is designed to **revise skills** that you might need in your assessed task. The selected content, outcomes, questions and answers are provided to help you to revise content and ways of applying your skills. Ask your tutor or check the **Pearson website** for the most up-to-date **Sample Assessment Material** and **Mark Scheme** to get an indication of the structure of your actual assessed task and what this requires of you. Pay attention to requirements in relation to how much time you have for different parts of the task, whether you can take any notes into the supervised assessment, whether you have access to a computer and any word limitations for written work. Notice how many marks are allocated to each activity. The details of the actual assessed task may change so always make sure you are up to date.

1 **Research and prepare in response to a brief (pages 61–82)**

- **Read** and **respond** to a brief that asks you to research, investigate and provide:
  - copy on two practitioners for an exhibition catalogue on a specified theme, with two images
  - a bibliography of your research sources
  - a letter explaining your judgement of which practitioner best interprets, exemplifies and communicates the theme and should appear at the start of the catalogue.

- Revise skills that are needed to investigate and research the two practitioners, selecting **one** out of two **specified practitioners** and **one** practitioner of **your choice**. The practitioner should be internationally recognised with an established reputation and presence whose work on the specified theme provides sufficient scope for in-depth contextual work and critical analysis.

- Revise skills that are needed to complete a **visual analysis** of a **supplied image** for the prescribed practitioner and of a **chosen piece** of work from your chosen practitioner. The visual analysis should show connections with contextual factors and theme, with copies of both images provided for the catalogue copy.

- Revise how to conduct a **thorough** investigation, including how the practitioners have addressed the theme in their work and contextual factors that have influenced them, enabling you to develop conclusions and form independent judgements. Give references for **primary** and **secondary sources** and a **bibliography**.

- Revise the skills involved when **writing** the catalogue copy, bibliography and letter:
  - to show quality and competence in your written communication and use of specialist terminology
  - to synthesise visual analysis and contextual factors to form judgements, compare practitioners and their work linked to the theme, and justify your arguments with evidence.

2 **Respond to activities, showing your ability in critical and contextual studies (pages 83–85)**

Consider how you will:

- prepare copy and images for the exhibition catalogue **and** your bibliography
- prepare your letter explaining which practitioner should appear at the start of the catalogue.

> **Links** To help you revise skills that might be needed in your Unit 2 assessed task this Workbook contains a revision task starting on page 55. See the introduction on page iii for more information on features included to help you revise.

Revision task

To support your revision, this Workbook contains a revision task to help you **revise the skills** that you might need in your assessed task. Ask your tutor or check the Pearson website for the up-to-date **Sample Assessment Material** and **Mark Scheme** to establish what is required of you. The details of the actual assessed task may change so always make sure you are up to date.

Revision task brief

Although you are given a revision brief that includes researching and producing copy in relation to an exhibition catalogue on the theme of 'Illusion', the activities in this Workbook will only require you to focus on the skills associated with the tasks. You are **not** expected to undertake full research, preparation and production of the copy for the catalogue, the bibliography, or the completed email and associated tasks. Although the theme in the revision brief is 'Illusion', the activities in this Workbook also involve a wider set of themes, images and internationally recognised practitioners to demonstrate skills that you can apply with any theme.

Start by reading the brief below.

A local gallery is hosting an exhibition of work by practitioners that have explored the theme of 'Illusion' in their work. It has asked you to contribute text and images to be included in a catalogue to support the exhibition. The catalogue must combine factual information, critical analysis and images to help visitors understand the artists and designers they will see in the exhibition.

You have been asked to select one of the following art and design practitioners to investigate and write copy on:

- M.C. Escher
- Bridget Riley.

Included in the catalogue must be a visual analysis of the image supplied in the revision task information (pages 58–60) for the practitioner you have chosen to write about.

The gallery has also asked you to select a second practitioner of your own choice who addresses the theme of 'Illusion' in their work to include in the catalogue.

The gallery has provided a briefing sheet on the theme of the exhibition and the images that have been selected for the guide. This can be found on pages 58–60.

Research and preparatory stage

Before completing revision activities 1 and 2 you must undertake research and preparation.

> Ask your tutor or check the up-to-date Sample Assessment Material on the Pearson website to find out how many hours you have for research and preparation in your actual assessment. Make sure you plan so that you complete the work within the allocated time. Pay attention to details, such as whether you can take notes from your research stage into your assessed activities, and any restrictions on the content, format and extent of notes, if so.

In preparation for the activities you must carry out an investigation into **one** of the following prescribed practitioners:

- M.C. Escher
- Bridget Riley.

You must also choose **one** additional practitioner to investigate who you believe deals with the theme of 'Illusion' in their work.

NB: Your chosen additional practitioner must:

- be recognised internationally, with an established reputation and presence
- provide sufficient scope for in-depth contextual work and critical analysis.

You must complete a visual analysis of the image supplied in the revision task information for your prescribed practitioner (pages 58–60) and for one piece of work from the practitioner you have chosen to investigate. You must supply copies of each of these images to include with your copy.

Your investigations should be thorough to enable you to develop conclusions and form independent judgements.

Revision activities

Although the revision task refers to producing copy with two images relating to the theme 'Illusion' for an exhibition catalogue plus a bibliography for revision activity 1 and a letter for revision activity 2, this Workbook will only require you to focus on the associated skills within a practical revision timeframe. Ask your tutor or check the Sample Assessment Material on the Pearson website to establish what is required in your actual assessment and how many hours you have for your assessed activities so that you can complete them within the allocated time. Pay attention to details such as whether you can refer to any of your research notes and any restrictions if so, and whether there is a word limit for each activity.

Revision activity 1

Prepare copy to be included in the catalogue for the exhibition 'Illusion'. Your copy must include information on:

- **either** M.C. Escher **or** Bridget Riley
- **one** additional practitioner of your choice.

The copy must include:

- the contextual factors that have influenced the practitioners and their work
- how the practitioners have addressed the issue of 'Illusion' in their work
- a visual analysis of two pieces of art and design work, one from each of the practitioners you have investigated.

You must also produce a bibliography of the research sources you used throughout your investigation. This should include both primary and secondary sources.

Make sure you show:

- the **quality** of your research material and how you used it to inform your understanding of the practitioners and their work and the contextual factors that have influenced them
- the **quality** of the visual analysis of the images and the connections with contextual factors and theme
- the **competence** and **quality** of your written communication and use of specialist terminology.

Revision activity 2

Prepare a covering letter to the curator of the exhibition explaining your judgement of which of the two practitioners you investigated best interprets, exemplifies and communicates the theme of 'Illusion' and should appear at the start of the catalogue.

You should put forward a balanced argument with justifications for your opinions and your conclusions.

Make sure you show your **ability** to:

- synthesise the visual analysis and contextual factors to form judgements
- compare the practitioners and their work linked to the theme
- justify your arguments with relevant evidence.

Revision task information

This revision task information is used as an example to show the skills you need. The content of a task will be different each year and the format may be different. Ask your tutor or check the latest Sample Assessment Material on the Pearson website for more details.

Briefing sheet

Below is the text that will be used in the introduction section of the catalogue about the theme 'Illusion'.

Theme: Illusion

Art and design practitioners have referenced 'Illusion' across different locations and ages. They have pursued the ability and potential in art and design to create illusions that can pose questions and ask viewers to reconsider their preconceived ideas and perceptions on the human condition. Artists have worked with surrealism, exploring the ability of media to convince us that the unreal might be real, or pushed our recognition of colour and shape, as in op art. They have explored reality by weaving elements of illusion into it. Designers have created objects that explore illusion in space, shape and scale. They have used design elements to create the illusion of space in environments, products and interiors. In commercial settings, some photographic practice relies heavily on using light and setting to create an illusion of something that is not there. Where digital editing has been used, this has sometimes caused controversy where illusions have been created and the truth distorted. Graphic designers, animators and filmmakers use illusion throughout their work to convince, cajole and inspire their audiences in a variety of ways.

Below are two of the practitioners who will be included in the exhibition, M.C. Escher and Bridget Riley, and the piece of their work that will be exhibited.

You must choose **one** of these artists to investigate and include in the catalogue.

Practitioner number one: M.C. Escher

Selected image: M.C. Escher's "Symmetry Drawing E126" © 2018 The M.C. Escher Company-The Netherlands. All rights reserved. www.mcescher.com

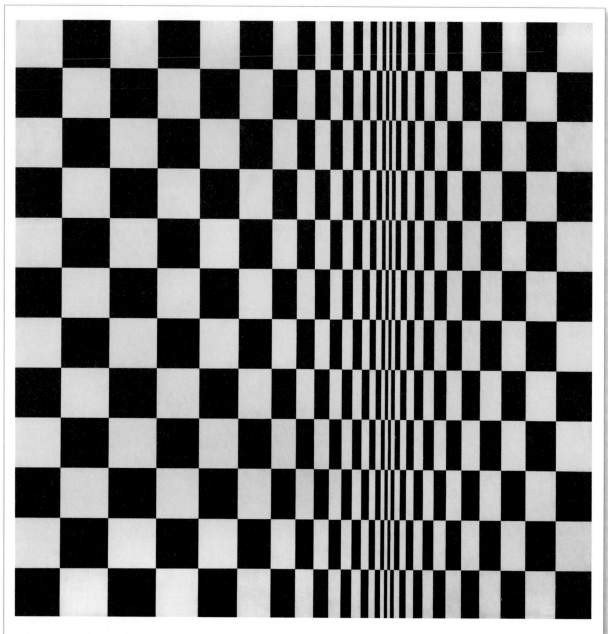

Practitioner number two: Bridget Riley

Selected image: 'Movement in Squares', 1961, Tempera on hardboard, 123.2 × 121.2 cm | 48 ½ × 47 ¾ © Bridget Riley 1961

(Source: Arts Council Collection, Southbank Centre, www.artuk.org)

Planning an investigation

When **reading** and **responding** to a brief that requires you to use contextual research and visual analysis in order to critically analyse the work of art and design practitioners related to a specified theme, consider the **requirements of the brief**.

> **Contextual influences** can be defined as the impact of other factors on a creative practitioner's work such as the time or era that work was produced, or any political, social and cultural influences.
>
> **Critical analysis** can be defined as a subjective piece of writing which expresses the writer's opinion or evaluation of a piece of work.

> Read the brief on pages 55–60 carefully. Then use the activities below that help to plan good quality research and investigation.

> **Links** To revise planning the investigation process, see pages 41–49 of the Revision Guide.

Guided **1** Complete the mind map of what you need to find out for an investigation.

The prescribed work

My own choice of their work

Ideas from the provided catalogue introduction

My choice of prescribed practitioner

My own choice of an internationally recognised practitioner

The theme

Practitioners and their works

Investigation plans – find out about

Ways that the two practitioners and their works relate to the theme

A range of relevant and reliable research sources

Primary sources such as

....

Secondary sources such as

....

Sources of contextual factors that influenced the practitioners/their

work such as ....

Guided **2** It is important to plan the investigation process. Complete an outline plan in relation to the brief, below.

Intention: In this contextual investigation I am researching ....

....

Clear aims: I want to find out ....

....

Clear objectives: I will research from primary sources by ....

....I will research from secondary sources by ....

....

I will research about contextual influences by ....

Timescale and action plans (specific, measurable, achievable, realistic and time-related): ....

....

Methods to record and collate findings and bibliography: I will ....

....

Using annotation

As part of your investigation into design practitioners and their work you will need to set up methods to record and collate information. You can use **written** and **visual annotation techniques** when working with a piece of art and design. The example below shows annotations in relation to deconstructing a piece of art and design work as part of visual analysis to show what has been discovered.

Guided 1 Look at the image and annotations below, related to a theme of 'Icons'. Analyse the image and add any initial annotations of your own.

This piece features a simplified image of the portrait of Marilyn Monroe using bright, flat colours and overprinted detail.

The image of the face changes as the series of images progress. There are variations in the colour and tonal ranges – like a photocopier. There are also distorted tones in the black and white half of the image.

The piece uses a low-grade newspaper-type image and coloration that seems harsh and artificial. It moves from colour to black and white, to almost a fade out at the far right. This image was used in the publicity pictures from Monroe's 1953 film, *Niagara*.

Marilyn Diptych, 1962. Andy Warhol.

Synthetic polymer paint and silkscreen ink on canvas

82 × 57 inches each (two panels)

© The Andy Warhol Foundation for the Visual Arts, Inc. / DACS/Artimage 2018

www.artimage.org.uk

The piece seems to be reducing the person in the image to a symbolic representation that the American public would have been aware of following Marilyn Monroe's death a few months earlier. Monroe's image was repeatedly shown as part of the reporting of her death.

....
....
....
....
....
....
....
....

2 Choose an image from page 59 or 60 in relation to the theme 'Illusion' or a key piece of art and design work related to a theme of your choice. Place a copy of it below and use annotations to record briefly some initial visual analysis of the piece of work.

When carrying out visual analysis, you can deconstruct art and design work through:
- **formal elements**: tonal values, colour, texture, pattern, form, shape, line, technical details
- **visual language**: scale, size, composition, viewpoint, framing medium, materials, process, production methods, techniques, other elements (use of text, time based, series)
- **visual communication**: subject matter, imagery, message, explicit and implicit messages/meanings, symbols and symbolism, intended mood and emotional impact, aesthetics, consideration of alternative readings or opinions about the work.

Annotating a piece of art and design work

....

....

....

....

....

....

....

Links To revise annotating imagery, see page 50 of the Revision Guide.

Organising your notes

Organising your notes is an important part of setting up methods to record and collate information found throughout the investigation. Use of research folders, notebooks, blogs and sketchbooks will help you organise your notes and visuals into an **ordered body** of research. Make sure you **cross-reference** information so you can locate and access it easily, and identify your sources using a recognised **referencing system**.

> Use the activities below to consider an organised approach for your notes. You can refer to notes you have made in relation to the theme 'Illusion', 'Icons' or any work you have completed.

Guided

1 Explain what you consider to be the best way of organising your notes, and why.

> You could use a format for grouping your notes, for example using a plan or index for key headings such as practitioner A, practitioner B, contextual factors, contextual influences, and so on.

I will need to use headings for my notes and research. I will include the following key points as

headers: ....

....

.... I will make sure I cross-reference my

work by ....

....

Guided

2 Give an example of how you will style references for each of the types of sources below, and explain the style for the bibliography.

> You must identify **primary** and **secondary** sources to use in your research and reference them with your notes and in a bibliography. You should use a recognised method, such as the Harvard system.

The recognised system to reference my

sources uses the following conventions, for example:

Style for books: ....

Style for journal articles: ....

Style for websites: ....

....

Style for bibliography: ....

....

Style for primary sources: ....

....

Guided

3 Explain how you will record your personal thoughts and reflections on a regular basis. Give an example of your reflections so far.

I will regularly record personal thoughts and reflections by ....

....When reflecting on ....

....

> **⌖ Links** To revise recording and collating information and organising your notes, see pages 44 and 51 of the Revision Guide.

Writing for scenarios

You will need to use your contextual research in a range of vocational scenarios. For example, with the scenario in the brief on pages 55–60 you would need to contribute copy to an exhibition catalogue and write a letter to the curator proposing which practitioner should be placed first in the catalogue and why.

When you write for different scenarios, you will need to select relevant content from your research and present it in a way that is appropriate for the format, purpose and audience.

> Examples of use of contextual research in vocational scenarios:
> - Developing content/information for magazine article
> - Content for online artist pages, info/graphics for exhibitions
> - Onscreen guide/website/event/trade fair/leaflet for an exhibit
> - Exhibition proposals and statements
> - Personal statements for competitions, shows or exhibitions
> - Interactive guide
> - Preparing for interviews
> - Commissions/briefs
> - Pitches

Guided

1. The spidergram below includes factors useful to consider when writing for scenarios.

   (a) Look at the scenario of writing exhibition copy in the brief on pages 55-60. Tick the questions below that would be relevant to consider in relation to the exhibition copy.

   (b) Jot down answers to the questions you have ticked in relation to the exhibition copy.

   (c) Complete the summary on page 66.

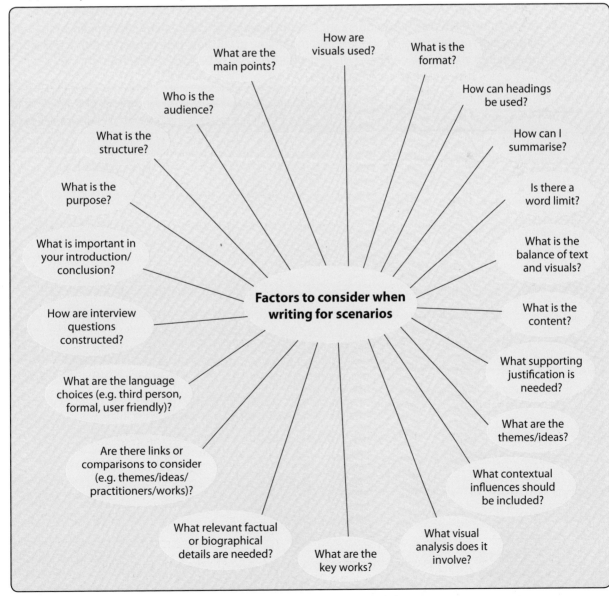

Factors to consider when writing for scenarios:
- How are visuals used?
- What is the format?
- What are the main points?
- Who is the audience?
- How can headings be used?
- What is the structure?
- How can I summarise?
- What is the purpose?
- Is there a word limit?
- What is important in your introduction/conclusion?
- What is the balance of text and visuals?
- How are interview questions constructed?
- What is the content?
- What are the language choices (e.g. third person, formal, user friendly)?
- What supporting justification is needed?
- Are there links or comparisons to consider (e.g. themes/ideas/practitioners/works)?
- What are the themes/ideas?
- What relevant factual or biographical details are needed?
- What contextual influences should be included?
- What are the key works?
- What visual analysis does it involve?

The purpose of an exhibition catalogue is to ....

....

....

The language choice will be third person, for example 'Graphic designers, animators and

filmmakers use illusion throughout their work to convince, cajole and inspire their audiences

in a variety of ways'. When considering whether the style should be formal or informal

....

....

The audience might include specialists and non-specialists, so it will be important to ....

.... Some catalogue entries have a limit of, for example, around

1800 words, so it is important to ....

.... I will use headings to give a logical structure to the catalogue

entry and ensure a balance of text and visuals so that ....

....

2 Use your notes to plan what you might include in an introductory paragraph for an exhibition
catalogue. You can use practitioners and the theme of 'Illusion' (see pages 55–60), 'Icons' or a different
practitioner and theme you have worked with. These may be some initial thoughts only.

> When writing for scenarios, it is useful to compare a few examples of the kind of outcome required, to get a
> clear idea of what works well. Refer to the extract from the catalogue in the brief on page 58, for one example.

....

....

....

....

....

....

....

....

....

....

....

....

> **Links** To revise writing for scenarios, see pages 52–56 of the Revision Guide.

Writing justifications

You will need to justify your judgements, opinions and conclusions when communicating your contextual research about practitioners and their works. You should **support** and **explain** why the points you put forward are valid. This is an important part of your research and investigation to consider and include in your notes.

> Use the activities below to help you plan ways of writing justifications.

1 Start by selecting a practitioner that you believe works in a specific way with a theme. This can relate to 'Illusion', 'Icons' or any theme or pathway but you must be able to come up with responses about their work.

Selected practitioner: ....

> Use the mind map below to help you plan and write strong justifications.
>
> Use language and terminology appropriately.
>
> Reference information correctly.
>
> Ensure good quality of written communication.
>
> **Communicating and justifying conclusions and judgements**
>
> Offer structured arguments, conclusions and judgements justified with examples.
>
> Express opinions with reasoning.
>
> Clarify and explain points.

2 Write out **key words and phrases** to explain and define a selected practitioner's use of formal elements, visual language and visual communication (see page 63). Use the **correct terminology** accurately. These may be some initial thoughts only.

- Formal elements: ....

  ....

- Visual language: ....

  ....

- Visual communication: ....

  ....

3 Write sentences using **clear language**, **examples** and **quotations** to explain how you feel the practitioner addresses a theme in their work. These may be some initial thoughts only.

> For example:
> Kehinde Wiley's icons challenge the so-called canons of painting. Wiley believes viewers of his work are forced to ask, what are these guys doing? They are assuming the poses of colonial masters, the former bosses of the Old World. Wiley deliberately forces the viewer to confront his or her expectations about the associations with these images.

....

....

....

....

4 Use your notes to plan what you might include in a concluding paragraph for the letter in the scenario in the brief on pages 55–60. **Sum up** some main points of why a practitioner should appear first in the catalogue, justifying your judgements, views and opinions. You could use your work in relation to the theme of 'Illusion', 'Icons' or another theme you have worked with. These may be some initial thoughts only.

State the conclusion and justify it. For example: I would argue that Andy Warhol is a convincing choice to lead the catalogue, as his work has established itself as recognisable across a range of genres that explore the way that much of contemporary life is based on illusions of some sort or other...

If supporting a view or opinion, you could also use tentative language such as 'could be interpreted as' or 'may'.

....
....
....
....
....
....
....
....
....
....
....
....
....
....
....
....
....
....
....
....
....
....
....

Links To revise writing justifications, see pages 89–93 of the Revision Guide.

Considering themes and ideas

When responding to a brief such as the one on pages 55–60, you will need to research and consider how practitioners address themes (for example, Illusion) and the ideas or messages they are trying to convey (for example, challenging viewers to consider perceptions of reality). Some themes and ideas may link to contextual influences such as the time or era that work was produced or political, social and cultural influences.

Use the activities below to summarise three themes in the work of two practitioners, and the ideas or messages they were trying to communicate. You could use the theme of 'Illusion' or 'Icons' or any practitioners and themes you have worked with.

1 Summarise **three** themes and ideas in the work of your selected practitioner 1.

....

....

....

....

....

....

....

....

....

....

....

2 Summarise **three** themes and ideas in the work of your selected practitioner 2.

....

....

....

....

....

....

....

....

....

....

 Links To revise themes and ideas, see pages 57 and 62 of the Revision Guide.

Understanding contextual influences

During your investigation you will need to consider and analyse how contextual factors have influenced a creative practitioner's work. When you are choosing a practitioner to investigate, make sure there are sufficient sources for your research and that the practitioner is internationally recognised.

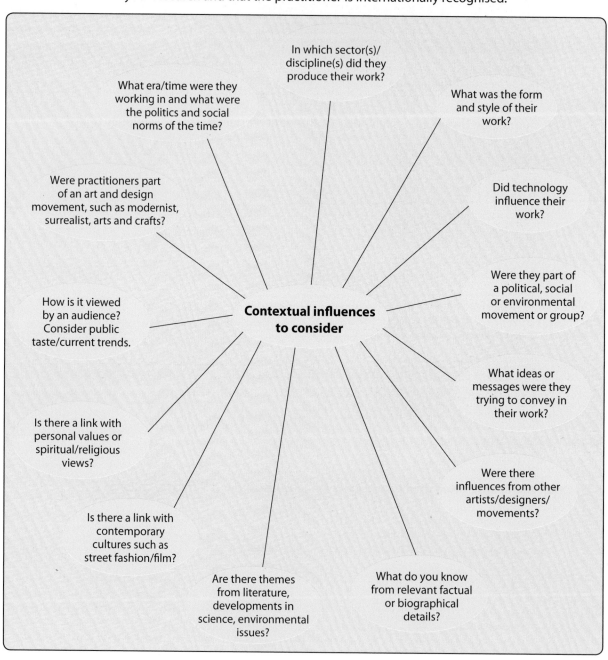

In which sector(s)/discipline(s) did they produce their work?

What era/time were they working in and what were the politics and social norms of the time?

What was the form and style of their work?

Were practitioners part of an art and design movement, such as modernist, surrealist, arts and crafts?

Did technology influence their work?

Contextual influences to consider

Were they part of a political, social or environmental movement or group?

How is it viewed by an audience? Consider public taste/current trends.

What ideas or messages were they trying to convey in their work?

Is there a link with personal values or spiritual/religious views?

Were there influences from other artists/designers/movements?

Is there a link with contemporary cultures such as street fashion/film?

Are there themes from literature, developments in science, environmental issues?

What do you know from relevant factual or biographical details?

1 Use the questions above to help you investigate the impact of at least **two** contextual influences on **one** of the practitioners and images on page 71, **or** your own choice. Note key findings from your research on page 72.

My choice of work and artist is ....

....

....

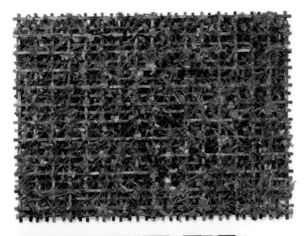

Contextual influences can vary due to the purpose and field that the art and design work addresses.

Michael Brennand-Wood, *Meshes*, 2012. Michael Brennand-Wood explores the theme of meshes and constructions in his work.

(Source: brennand-wood.com)

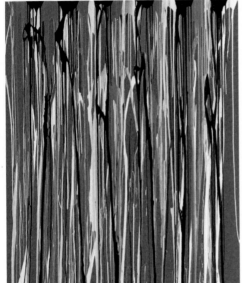

Contextual influences can reference urban detail and medium.

Ian Davenport, Untitled, 1989.

Household paint on canvas

72 × 60 in / 182.9 × 152.4 cm

© Ian Davenport. All Rights Reserved, DACS/Artimage 2018

This painting works on a number of different levels at the same time, referencing an earlier way of working.

(Source: artimage.org.uk)

> **Guided**

2 Choose a visual that supports your contextual research findings for your selected piece of work, and explain why.

My choice of visual that supports my contextual findings is ....

....

....

....

....

....

....

3 Note below the references for the sources for your contextual research.

....

....

....

....

Links See page 64 of this Workbook for how to reference your sources, using a system such as Harvard.

4 Use a mind map to gather your notes on the impact of contextual influences on the creative practitioner's work that you have identified and investigated.

> Visual diagrams can help you to get an overview of the impact of different contextual influences. You can also show links between points by drawing arrows between them.

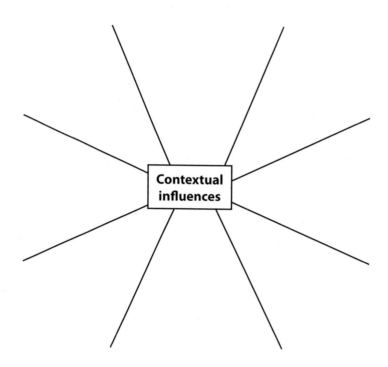

Contextual influences

5 Create a summary of the impact of contextual influences on the creative practitioner's work that you have investigated.

> Include explanations and examples in your summary.

....
....
....
....
....
....
....
....
....

> **Links** To revise the impact of contextual factors on practitioners and their works, see pages 57–67 of the Revision Guide.

Investigating key works

When responding to a brief such as the one on pages 55–60, you will need to complete a **visual analysis** of one work supplied for the prescribed practitioner and one piece of work from a practitioner you have chosen to investigate, showing the connections with contextual factors and theme. It is important to choose a **key work** that exemplifies the practitioner, investigating a few key works before you select the one you will analyse.

> As part of the contextual influence on key works you will need to consider:
> • the purpose of the key works, such as to exhibit, for a magazine/publication
> • the practitioners' use of visual language, formal elements and imagery
> • themes in the practitioners' work
> • use of materials, techniques and processes.

Guided

1 Use the points on this page to identify a key work you would choose by an internationally recognised practitioner that relates to the theme of 'Illusion', 'Icons' or another theme that you have worked with.

> A key work is one that can be said to be representative of a practitioner's or brand's output, or marks a turning point or breakthrough.

You will also deconstruct this piece of art and design work through formal elements, visual language and visual communication on pages 74–77.

The key work I have identified is ....

....

....

2 Explain why the work you have chosen is a key work.

....

....

....

....

....

....

....

....

....

....

....

....

....

> **Links** To revise the investigation of key works by a practitioner, see pages 68–70 of the Revision Guide.

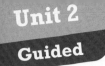

Deconstructing formal elements

Your **visual analysis** of a prescribed work and a chosen work as required by the brief on pages 55–60 will involve you in **deconstructing** art and design work, including formal elements.

> **Formal elements**: tonal values, colour, texture, pattern, form, shape, line, technical details (e.g. measurements, medium, title).

1 Using the key work you have chosen on page 73 by an internationally recognised practitioner in relation to the theme of 'Illusion', 'Icons' or another theme you have worked with, list the formal elements that have been used in your chosen piece.

....

....

....

....

....

....

2 Use analysis to identify how formal elements have been used to communicate themes and ideas in this piece.

....

....

....

....

....

....

....

....

....

....

....

....

....

....

....

> • Analysing each formal element will help you to identify the components of the work so you can gain an insight into the choices that have been made and the thinking behind the piece.
> • Pay attention to how the formal elements overlap and reinforce each other, combining to communicate visually. How do they communicate the themes and ideas, and link to any contextual factors?
> • You can refine your deconstruction over time and make it more in-depth, noticing detail beyond the obvious.
> • Your analysis of formal elements will help to develop your awareness of the similarities and differences when comparing works of art and design by different practitioners.

> **Links** To revise analysis of formal elements, see pages 71–73 of the Revision Guide.

Deconstructing visual language

You will need to **deconstruct visual language** in your prescribed work and a chosen work of art and design as required by the brief on pages 55–60, showing any connections with contextual factors and theme.

Visual language:
- Scale, size
- Composition, viewpoint, framing medium
- Materials
- Process
- Production methods
- Other elements used in visual language: use of text, time based, series

Some aspects in visual language may be linked very closely to contextual influences.

1 Using the key work you have chosen on page 73 by an internationally recognised practitioner in relation to the theme of 'Illusion', 'Icons' or another theme you have worked with, describe how visual language is used in this piece. You will need to research some of these aspects using secondary sources through literature or the internet. Make sure that you reference your sources.

- When deconstructing visual language, you are thinking about the message in the work – understanding the intention and the ways it is communicated. There may be many possible interpretations and responses when reading a piece of work.
- Show that you know how to separate components of visual work by picking out examples of the different aspects of visual language. It is natural that aspects of formal elements, visual language and visual communication may overlap when deconstructing visual language.
- Start by describing what you see, then focus on details to narrow down your analysis.

....

....

....

....

....

....

....

....

....

....

....

....

....

....

....

....

....

....

2 Use visual diagrams or studies to support your deconstruction of visual language in your chosen piece of art and design. You could use annotations for your analysis.

Consider different approaches to using visuals, for example:
- **photographs** in galleries to record primary sources where relevant and permitted
- **line drawings** to show the basic components and composition in a work
- **isolation of detail** to examine specific components of visual language
- **highlighting contextual influences** on the work.

Deconstructing visual language – visual diagrams or studies to support my analysis

 Links To revise deconstructing visual language, see pages 74–76 of the Revision Guide.

Deconstructing visual communication

You will need to **deconstruct visual communication** in your prescribed work and a chosen work of art and design as required by the brief on pages 55–60, showing any connections with contextual factors and theme.

> **Visual communication**: subject matter, imagery, message, explicit and implicit messages and/or meanings, symbols and symbolism, intended mood and emotional impact, aesthetics, consideration of alternative readings or opinions about the work.

1 Using the key work you have chosen on page 73 by an internationally recognised practitioner in relation to the theme of 'Illusion', 'Icons' or another theme you have worked with, research and develop your analysis to show how visual communication is used in this piece. Make sure that you reference your sources.

> • Consider each of the aspects of visual communication in relation to the work. Look at the details and the ways they connect. You will need to reference formal elements and visual language to do this.
> • Develop your understanding of the work and what you think it's about (its meaning) and what it's trying to say (its message) and how it is doing this.
> • When reaching conclusions, consider what you have learned about the work you have researched, what factors the practitioners have explored, and how they have communicated this to you.

(a) How has the practitioner used visual communication to highlight a theme in the work?

....

....

....

....

....

....

....

(b) How has the practitioner used visual communication to communicate message(s) or meaning(s)?

....

....

....

....

....

....

....

> **Links** To revise deconstructing visual communication, see pages 77–81 of the Revision Guide.

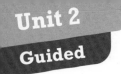

Summarising key information

You will need to **summarise key information** as you **draw conclusions and form judgements** on the research that you have carried out. The information you use will need to be relevant when responding to a brief such as that on pages 55–60 with a scenario, such as contributing copy to an exhibition catalogue, and explaining which practitioner should lead the catalogue.

> **Guided**

1 Complete the table to identify and summarise key information for the practitioner and the key piece of art and design that you investigated on pages 73–77, or another practitioner and piece of work that you have investigated and know well. Add entries if there is further key information to include.

When summarising key information:
- select relevant and reliable information – review all the information before you decide what to use
- identify key points – ensure your research notes do this so you have a good idea of what the key points are
- present findings and conclusions – use a combination of written and visual information.

You can use headings and bullet points to structure your summary, and cross references where one piece of research can be used more than once. Use specialist terminology correctly. You may find it useful to summarise using a table. You can then add a column for practitioner 2 which is useful for comparisons.

Theme: ....

Key points	Practitioner 1: .... Key piece of art and design: ....
Influence of contextual factors on the work and practice of the practitioner	•
How the practitioner has addressed the theme in the work	•
Visual analysis, showing connections between: • formal elements	•

• visual language	•
• visual communication	•
• contextual sources	•
Research sources	•

My visual summaries to support the findings and conclusions in the key points

Links To revise summarising key information, see page 83 of the Revision Guide.

Making connections

Making **connections** between messages, themes, creative intentions and the visual elements that form a work will help you to form **independent judgements** that support your conclusions.

> When you are making connections across all your research, make sure you **select** what is **relevant** to form judgements that support your conclusions. Explain your interpretations, using examples, quotations and factual evidence to reinforce your views. Make sure you reference your sources.

1   Make connections across the research you have carried out on **two practitioners** relating to the same theme in order to outline some key ways they have approached and represented the theme in their work.

    ....

    ....

    ....

    ....

    ....

    ....

    ....

    ....

    ....

    ....

2   Make connections across the research you have carried out on a **key work** by each practitioner to support your views above. Include a quotation.

> Make the connections work by keeping them specific.

    ....

    ....

    ....

    ....

    ....

    ....

    ....

    ....

    ....

    ....

> **Links** To revise making links and connections, see pages 84–85 of the Revision Guide.

Making comparisons and links

You will need to **make comparisons** and **links to other work** as you draw conclusions and form independent judgements on the research that you have carried out. The comparisons you make will need to be relevant when responding to a brief such as that on pages 55–60 with a scenario such as explaining which of two practitioners in your judgement should lead in an exhibition catalogue.

> You will need to summarise the key points of your comparison. The points you select will need to support your judgement and conclusions. Using a table to compare key points with two practitioners can be useful, for example extending the table on pages 78–79 with an extra column for practitioner 2.

> Use your analysis and research to judge which of your researched practitioners best exemplifies or communicates the theme in your judgement, by completing the activities below. The work on pages 78–80 should support this comparison.

1 Define the theme, and decide which practitioner in your judgement best exemplifies or communicates this theme. Base this on your visual analysis and research, including links to other work.

....

....

....

....

....

....

2 Explain the key points of this judgement in more detail, using appropriate terminology and referencing **one** key piece of art and design by each practitioner. Include a quotation to support your judgement.

> You can develop justifications by referring to key works, using examples and quotations, applying visual analysis with consideration of contextual factors, and deciding on visual impact. To show analysis you can discuss similarities and differences.

....

....

....

....

....

....

....

....

....

....

....

> **Links** To revise comparing practitioners, see pages 82, 86–87 of the Revision Guide.

Justifying conclusions

When you have made judgements and conclusions as a result of your investigation, you need to communicate and justify them. To justify your conclusons you need to support them. Be clear about the points you make.

Use language and terminology appropriately when referring to formal elements, materials, techniques, processes and concepts.

Reference information correctly – use a referencing convention for your primary and secondary sources and contextual references, and compile a bibliography of your sources.

Ensure good quality of written communication – your writing should be formal, avoid slang or abbreviations, use the third person, remain succinct and avoid repetition.

Communicate and justify conclusions and judgements

Clarify and explain points – identify key points and communicate how they are relevant.

Express opinions with reasoning – your viewpoint is important and you can support it with examples and relevant quotations.

Offer structured arguments, conclusions and judgements justified with examples – summarise key points, make connections and link your points.

Guided

1 From your investigation, complete the points below in relation to the brief on pages 55–60.

Three key areas I need to consider when forming and justifying conclusions and judgements in relation to copy to be included in an exhibition catalogue are:

* Defining the theme and explaining ....

* Comparing and contrasting ....

* Summarising information and ....

Three key aspects I need to consider when putting forward a balanced argument with justification for my opinions and conclusions in relation to who should appear at the start of the catalogue are:

* How I identified ....

* Key works that ....

* Supporting evidence from others such as ....

When making justifications, it is important to support them by including/using:

* Relevant quotations, such as ....

....

* Visual analysis, such as ....

....

* References and bibliography, such as ....

....

2 Use the spidergram above to check how far your work shows these qualities. Tick the ones you feel confident about. If there are any that you need to improve, note how you will do this.

 Links To revise communicating and justifying conclusions and judgements, see pages 88–93 of the Revision Guide.

Revision activities

Although the revision task refers to producing copy with two images relating to the theme 'Illusion' for an exhibition catalogue plus a bibliography for revision activity 1 and a letter for revision activity 2, this Workbook will only require you to focus on the associated skills within a practical revision timeframe.

Ask your tutor or check the Sample Assessment Material on the Pearson website to establish what is required in your actual assessment and how many hours you have for your assessed activities so that you can complete them within the allocated time. Pay attention to details such as whether you can refer to any notes, and limitations if so, and whether there is a word limit for each activity.

Revision activity 1

Prepare copy to be included in the catalogue for the exhibition 'Illusion'. Your copy must include information on:

- **either** M.C. Escher **or** Bridget Riley
- **one** additional practitioner of your choice.

The copy must include:

- the contextual factors that have influenced the practitioners and their work
- how the practitioners have addressed the issue of 'Illusion' in their work
- a visual analysis of two pieces of art and design work, one from each of the practitioners you have investigated.

For this revision activity you could instead work with a theme and two practitioners of your choice.

You must also produce a bibliography of the research sources you used throughout your investigation. This should include both primary and secondary sources.

Make sure you show:

- the **quality** of your research material and how you used it to inform your understanding of the practitioners and their work and the contextual factors that have influenced them
- the **quality** of the visual analysis of the images and the connections with contextual factors and theme
- the **competence** and **quality** of your written communication and use of specialist terminology.

For your actual assessment, notice if any word limits apply to the copy, for example up to 1800 words.

1 Create an outline plan of your response in relation to the theme of 'Illusion', 'Icons' or any theme you have worked with. Include key headings and a brief summary of what you think is important for the different parts of your response.

2 Explain the conventions you will use when compiling your bibliography.

You could use a flow diagram to show your outline plan visually.

....

....

....

....

....

....

Revision activity 2

Prepare a covering letter to the curator of the exhibition explaining your judgement of which of the two practitioners you investigated best interprets, exemplifies and communicates the theme of 'Illusion', 'Icons' or any theme you have worked with, and should appear at the start of the catalogue.

You should put forward a balanced argument with justifications for your opinions and your conclusions.

Make sure you show your **ability** to:

- synthesise the visual analysis and contextual factors to form judgements
- compare the practitioners and their work linked to the theme
- justify your arguments with relevant evidence.

For your actual assessment, notice if any word limits apply to the letter, for example up to 400 words.

Create an outline plan of your response. Include headings and a brief summary of what you think is important for the different parts of your response. You could use a flow diagram to show your outline plan visually.

....

....

....

....

....

....

....

....

....

....

....

....

....

....

....

....

....

....

....

....

Unit 6: Managing a Client Brief

Your set task

Unit 6 will be assessed through a task, which will be set by Pearson. You will need to use your understanding of responding to a client brief in the art and design sector by researching the client, developing your ideas, and producing a presentation for the client that demonstrates your ideas in response to the brief.

Your Revision Workbook

This Workbook is designed to **revise skills** that you might need in your assessed task. The selected content, outcomes, questions and answers are provided to help you to revise content and ways of applying your skills. Ask your tutor or check the **Pearson website** for the most up-to-date **Sample Assessment Material** and **Mark Scheme** to get an indication of the structure of your actual assessed task and what this requires of you. Pay attention to requirements in relation to how much time you have for different parts of the task, whether you can take any preparatory work into the supervised assessment and whether you have access to a computer. The details of the actual assessed task may change so always make sure you are up to date.

1 **Research and prepare in response to a client brief (pages 99–122)**
   - **Read** and **respond** to a client brief which requires you to research the client, develop ideas, and produce a presentation for the client that demonstrates your ideas.
   - **Revise skills** that are needed to:
     - use a client information pack as a starting point to research an organisation
     - select which of the 'big issues' to focus on for your designs and to research the issues
     - choose **one** of two target audiences: for example, young people aged 11–18 years **or** young adults aged 19–34 years
     - select **one** brief from **one** of the different specialisms listed in the client information pack
     - develop ideas in response to the brief you have selected
     - keep records and notes on the development of your designs made throughout this stage
     - select **one** idea to include in your presentation (this does not have to be a fully finished design)
     - develop a version of the presentation and accompanying speaker notes.

2 **Produce a presentation for the client that demonstrates your ideas in response to a client brief (page 123)**

   Consider how you will include in your presentation:
   - the target audience and big issue you have chosen to respond to
   - how you have selected and used the information from the client pack to inform your ideas
   - how you developed your ideas from the initial stages through to the final idea
   - your final idea in response to **one** of the client briefs
   - visual representation of your ideas
   - your choice of formal elements and materials, techniques and processes
   - how your ideas address the target audience you have selected
   - how your ideas address the big issue you have selected
   - justification of how your ideas meet the client brief.

   Links To help you revise skills that might be needed in your Unit 6 assessed task this Workbook contains a revision task starting on page 87. Activities to help you develop the skills needed for your task begin on page 99. See the introduction on page iii for more information on features included to help you revise.

Revision task

To support your revision, this Workbook contains a revision task to help you **revise the skills** that you might need in your assessed task. Ask your tutor or check the Pearson website for the up-to-date **Sample Assessment Material** and **Mark Scheme** to establish what is required of you. The details of the actual assessed task may change so always make sure you are up to date.

Revision task brief

Although you are given a revision brief that includes researching and producing a presentation to increase participation and support for Cancer Research UK, the activities in this Workbook will only require you to focus on the skills associated with the task. You are **not** expected to undertake full research, preparation and production of a presentation. Although the brief and associated tasks are specific to Cancer Research UK, the activities in this Workbook also allow you to demonstrate your skills in a wider context.

Start by reading the brief below.

Cancer Research UK is a registered charity offering information and a network of support and contacts about cancer. It wants to increase the participation of young people and young adults in its 'big issues' and introduce these demographics to the work of Cancer Research UK, in turn increasing the support from these age groups. It has a plan to include a stronger high street presence and further develop social media as a promotion tool for communication and fundraising. It is planning to launch a campaign targeting these groups and has a planned schedule of nationwide projects and events, taking place in high streets and hospitals throughout the summer months.

Ahead of the launch of the campaign, Cancer Research UK wants to develop a distinct identity for its visual materials and staff as part of its brand development process. This includes some of its literature, visual information, uniforms, props and marketing materials (physical and web based), and an interactive app that can link information, support and offer potential for instant fundraising. The design of these items should provide information and support, and an identifiable brand, as well as stressing the importance of fundraising to the organisation, notwithstanding the pressures on the target audiences' finances. It is targeting young people (11–18 years) and young adults (19–34 years).

Cancer Research UK would like to commission visual ideas for the visual designs for the launch of this campaign from art and design practitioners. Artists and designers are asked to produce a presentation of no more than 20 slides with their ideas in response to one of the briefs provided.

Cancer Research UK has produced a client pack that gives information on the organisation, the big issues it wants to address, the audiences it wants to target, and the specific design briefs that need responding to. This can be found on page 89.

You will pick **one** client brief from one of the following art and design disciplines:

- 3D Design
- Fashion
- Textiles
- Photography
- Fine Art
- Graphics
- Interactive Design

Please note that the content in this revision brief (pages 87–98) is for illustrative purposes, and some content provided by Cancer Research UK has been amended by the Publisher for the purposes of the brief. Cancer Research UK is independent from Pearson Education Ltd and a source of trusted information for all. The use of content linked to Cancer Research UK does not indicate that Cancer Research UK directly endorses Pearson Education Ltd or its products and services. The Publisher extends thanks to Cancer Research UK for their kind permission.

Researching the client and the development of ideas

> Ask your tutor or check the up-to-date Sample Assessment Material on the Pearson website to find out how many hours you have for research and preparation in your actual assessment. Make sure you plan so that you complete the work within the allocated time.

Ahead of putting together your presentation you must:
- use the client information pack as a starting point to research Cancer Research UK as an organisation
- select which of the 'big issues' you want to use as the focus for your designs and research the issue
- choose **one** of two target audiences: young people aged 11–18 years or young adults aged 19–34 years
- select **one** brief from **one** of the different specialisms listed in the client information pack
- develop ideas in response to the brief you have selected
- keep records and notes on the development of your designs made throughout this stage
- select **one** idea to include in your presentation (this does not have to be a fully finished design)
- develop a version of the presentation and accompanying speaker notes.

You need to show your ability to:
- select relevant information and material from the brief to inform ideas
- organise your presentation in a logical and professional way that covers all areas of the task and meets the requirements of the client brief
- communicate your ideas
- make links between the client requirements and your ideas
- explain how your ideas meet the brief
- justify your ideas.

Revision activities

Revision activity 1

> Ask your tutor or check the up-to-date Sample Assessment Material on the Pearson website to find out how many hours you have for the activity in your actual assessment. Make sure you plan so that you complete the work within the allocated time. Pay attention to details, such as whether you have access to a computer and whether you can take work from the research and preparation stage into your assessed activities.
>
> Although the revision brief includes researching and producing a presentation to increase participation and support for Cancer Research UK, the activities in this Workbook will only require you to focus on the skills associated with this activity. You are **not** expected to undertake full research, preparation and production of a presentation. Although the brief and associated tasks are specific to Cancer Research UK, the activities in this Workbook also allow you to demonstrate your skills in a wider context.

Produce a presentation for the client that demonstrates your ideas in response to a client brief.

Consider how you will include in your presentation:
- the target audience and big issue you have chosen to respond to
- how you have selected and used the information from the client pack to inform your ideas
- how you developed your ideas from the initial stages through to the final idea
- your final idea in response to **one** of the client briefs
- visual representation of your ideas
- your choice of formal elements and materials, techniques and processes
- how your ideas address the target audience you have selected
- how your ideas address the big issue you have selected
- justification of how your ideas meet the client brief.

The presentation should contain no more than 20 slides with accompanying speaker notes.

Revision task information

> This revision task information is used as an example to show the skills you need. The content of a task will be different each year and the format may be different. Ask your tutor or check the latest Sample Assessment Material on the Pearson website for more details.

Information about the client

CANCER RESEARCH UK

Our vision is to bring forward the day when all cancers are cured.

In the 1970s, less than a quarter of people with cancer survived. But over the last 40 years, survival has doubled – today half will survive.

Our ambition is to accelerate progress and see three-quarters of people surviving the disease within the next 20 years.

Our new strategy will give us the foundations we need to tackle the challenges ahead.

Tackling all cancers

We want survival in the UK to be among the best in the world. We're focusing our efforts in four key areas – working to help prevent cancer, diagnose it earlier, develop new treatments and optimise current treatments by personalising them and making them even more effective.

We'll continue to support research into all types of cancer and across all age groups. And we're keeping our focus on understanding the biology of cancer so we can use this vital knowledge to save more lives.

We're increasing our research in key areas such as early diagnosis, and hard-to-treat cancers including lung, pancreatic, oesophageal cancers and brain tumours.

We're developing new tests, surgery and radiotherapy techniques, and cancer drugs. We want to personalise prevention, screening and treatment and bring benefits to patients sooner.

To help accelerate progress, we'll be investing an additional £50 million a year into new funding schemes for our researchers. These will encourage collaboration and innovation, and support research tackling some of the biggest scientific challenges in cancer research.

Smoking is the biggest preventable cause of cancer and we'll work towards the day when no one in the UK smokes – in particular by protecting children and helping people to quit.

We'll campaign for the best cancer services in all parts of the UK, and give more people the chance to join the fight against cancer.

But we can't achieve our mission alone. We rely on our dedicated scientists, doctors and nurses, and the generosity of our supporters across the UK. With your help, we can beat cancer sooner.

The 'big issues' are:

o   providing accurate, supportive information about cancer

o   preventing cancer through addressing lifestyle risks

o   generating income to support cancer research through fundraising.

The big issues support the objectives of Cancer Research UK: to **prevent** – reducing people's risk of developing cancer; **diagnose** more cancers earlier; **treat** – develop new cancer treatments; **optimise** – make treatments more effective for each patient.

Cancer Research UK has provided a client information pack. This includes a short history of the business, website content, images and other details. You will use the client information pack as a starting point for your research, ideas generation and designs and devise a response to your selected brief and appropriate materials for the presentation.

Revision client briefs

Select one brief from one of the following specialisms.

3D Design

Pick **one** of the following:

1 Design an exhibition display for use in a Cancer Research UK high street shop.

OR

2 Design low-cost jewellery/body adornment that references Cancer Research UK for sale in fundraising.

OR

3 Design a puzzle/game that has an educational message linked to Cancer Research UK.

Fashion

Pick **one** of the following:

1 Design a series of three wearable accessories for Cancer Research UK staff.

OR

2 Design a costume for a fundraising event that promotes Cancer Research UK.

OR

3 Design a low-cost accessory that references Cancer Research UK that can be sold at fundraising events.

Fine Art

Pick **one** of the following:

1 Design a series of three printed images referencing Cancer Research UK, to be sold at a fundraising event.

OR

2 Design a portable sculptural piece that references Cancer Research UK.

OR

3 Design a set of illustrations that reference aspects of Cancer Research UK's history.

Graphics

Pick **one** of the following:

1 Design a series of three posters promoting Cancer Research UK.

OR

2 Design a new series of three brochure covers for Cancer Research UK publications.

OR

3 Design a piece of infographics on what Cancer Research UK offers, promoting awareness of its research.

Interactive Design

Pick **one** of the following:

1 Design a series of three linked pages of the Cancer Research UK website that address a key theme.

OR

2 Design a short interactive film or animation that promotes Cancer Research UK.

OR

3 Design an app for fundraising for Cancer Research UK.

Photography

Pick **one** of the following:

1 Plan a series of three images that show Cancer Research UK in a positive light.

OR

2 Plan a series of three images that could provide a narrative to an individual's relationship with Cancer Research UK.

OR

3 Plan a series of three images showing how cancer can affect anyone, regardless of gender, age, race and background.

Textiles

Pick **one** of the following:

1 Design a series of three surface patterns for cards, notebook covers and recyclable paper bags to be used and sold in Cancer Research UK shops.

OR

2 Design a series of three banners and hangings for the physical displays in a Cancer Research UK shop.

OR

3 Design a set of two pieces of constructed textiles that promote Cancer Research UK.

Company history and background

For more information: www.cancerresearchuk.org and search for 'research history'.

Our strategy:

To beat cancer sooner

Tackle cancer

Cancer Research UK is a British registered charity. We are involved in research, campaigning, supporting and developing strategies to tackle cancer in all its forms. In the 1970s less than a quarter of people with cancer survived. Today this has risen to 50%. We have ambitious targets to accelerate progress in seeking treatments through laboratory and fieldwork, so that 75% of people will survive cancer within 20 years from now. We have developed an ongoing response to raising awareness of the importance of research for treatments for cancer through early laboratory-based work. We have been involved in the work that identified hereditary components, and that tested life-saving treatments in patients such as radiotherapy and chemotherapy. We have links with many research organisations and we're involved at the cutting edge in this field. We also provide funding for research grants.

Campaign

We want to raise awareness of how lifestyle can affect a person's risk of developing cancer. We want to catch cancer before it gets a chance to develop, so we are targeting young people and raising their awareness of lifestyle issues. We also want to continue our ground-breaking work in campaigning and promoting research into the causes and treatments for cancers. We are the world's largest cancer support organisation, and we will use our influence to drive research forward with our partners.

Support

We are going to continue to offer support for people by helping them to make positive lifestyle choices to lower their risks of cancer. To do this we need to gain a solid understanding of what affects people by continuing our research with scientists into the causes and genetic markers for cancer, so we can identify it earlier and prevent it where possible.

Develop strategies

Our research work in science has improved our understanding of the factors that influence specific types of cancer. For instance, we know that our genes can affect our chances of developing breast or prostate cancer. We want to learn more about the links between environment, lifestyle, genetics and other factors so we can offer real preventative advice and guidance.

House Design Styles

Why is choosing the right image important?

We are often dealing with difficult situations. Cancer will affect one in two of us, yet there is still sometimes a reluctance to talk about it, especially in the older generation. This may be because it was seen as an incurable disease in the past, although we are helping to change that perception. Our images will say a great deal about cancer and how it affects people.

Cancer Research UK Imagery

The images we use are carefully chosen.

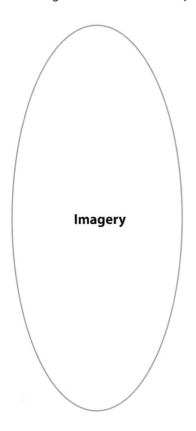

Imagery

We use photographs to show real life case studies of people affected by cancer. We use these images to show the human situations and to bring the issue of cancer to life. This provides a real-life context and justification to support our efforts in fundraising, research and raising awareness.

We know that cancer can be upsetting for people to come to terms with, so we hope our images of case studies can help other people with the disease to feel more positive in their outlook and the possibility of treatment.

We also use imagery to show the nature of our work. These images can include scientific images and diagrams to reference our work with scientists and laboratories. Some imagery may also be technical, to explain how cancer cells can develop. We use these images to try to demystify the disease, and show it just as any other disease – it has structure, and we know how it can grow, and we are using this knowledge to try and prevent it.

More information about elements of our visual identity, including our style guide and writers' guidelines, can be found here:

http://www.cancerresearchuk.org and search for 'about our information'.

Examples of Cancer Research UK work across the UK

Tackling cancer

We tackle cancer though trials that develop our understanding of the disease and how we can treat it. Each gain we make in our understanding brings us closer to being able to beat the disease head on and develop treatments that are effective. We have developed something called the Stratified Medicine Programme, using Drug Development Units and Drug Development Office to speed up how we support patients. We believe preventative methods can be further developed and can help in our aims to reduce young people's risk of developing cancer.

Logo and branding

Our logo is important: it is a symbol that stands for our identity and is known throughout the world. It can be seen in a variety of settings, not least in the high street. It uses a simple colour range, and is a recognisable brand. We have used straplines in the past such as 'let's beat cancer sooner'. In this brief, the strapline can be developed to be aimed at the target audience.

Developing strategies with website access to information

We know that young people use technology all the time, both at work and socially. We want to use this technology to reach out to them with our message. We also want to use the potential of technology on our websites both for information and as a way of encouraging prevention and early screening. We want young people to access the information and tools on the website to help them in this.

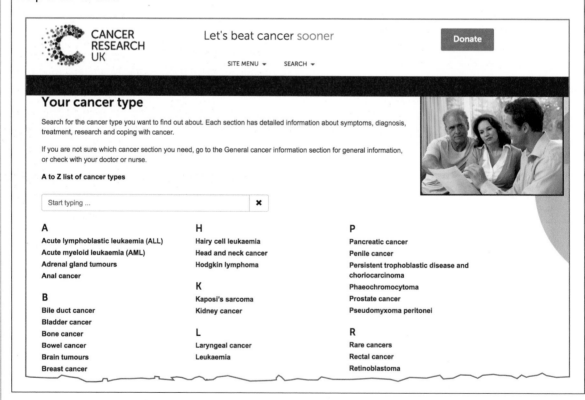

Examples of Cancer Research UK work across the UK

Supporting and campaigning for Cancer Research UK

We show real life people who have cancer, and use their stories to highlight the disease and to offer hope and support to others. We encourage volunteers, fundraising and events to raise our income, as surprisingly we don't receive any direct funding from the UK government. Nine out of ten donations we receive are for £10 or less, so it's vital we have as large a network of volunteers and people with us to make this all work. Last year 40,000 people volunteered to work with us.

Volunteering

We are always looking for volunteers to help at our local high street stores. There is probably one in the nearest town or city to you now. You can also donate items to the shop as another way of helping us raise funds. Our shops are often a focus for local fundraising events as well.

Cancer Research UK Big Issues

Providing accurate, supportive information about cancer

We work with scientists and the medical profession to provide information packs and leaflets/ website information on the different types of cancers. We think information is a key component in understanding how the disease works and how it can be treated.

People are living longer today. This means there is more chance of people developing age-related cancers as they grow older. A larger elderly population means more pressure on the health service. This makes it important that we all do what we can to remove as many factors from our lives that are linked to developing cancer. Providing clear information is an important part of this process.

Our leaflets and info packs are written in a clear and concise way. We want the information to be useful in understanding cancer. We have found the first step to tackling cancer is to find out about it and discuss this. We want our support materials to do just that – support.

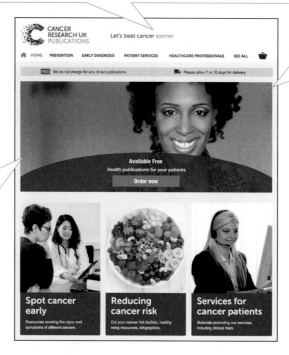

We have a network of people and organisations that concerned patients, family members and anyone worried about cancer can contact for support. The website is a key feature of this and we would like to expand its visual presence – we would like to have a set of visuals that addresses the different parts of our mission.

We can use information to raise people's self-awareness of cancer – nine out of ten people can be treated successfully for bowel cancer if it is spotted at the earliest stage, but fewer than one in ten cases are diagnosed at this point.

What is cancer?

A tumour is forming

Cancer cells dividing — Normal cells

Cancer Research UK

Cancer grows as cells multiply over and over

Cancer cells

Normal cells

Cancer starts when cells change abnormally

Cancer is when abnormal cells divide in an uncontrolled way.

Some cancers may eventually spread into other tissues.

There are more than 200 different types of cancer.

1 in 2 people in the UK will get cancer in their lifetime.

Thanks to research many people are cured.

▶ How does cancer start?

Cancer starts when gene changes make one cell or a few cells begin to grow and multiply too much. This may cause a growth called a tumour.

▶ How does cancer grow?

We want to use visuals to explain how all cancers are driven by DNA so-called 'mistakes'. These change the way the cell behaves. We know some cancers are inherited, but we believe most are caused by genetic faults that build up over time.

Cancer Research UK Big Issues

Preventing cancer through addressing lifestyle risks

We know now that some activities can be triggers for cancers. Decades of research have given us information that we can now use with some certainty to inform people of risks associated with certain lifestyle choices. We want people to choose to change, in order to prevent the disease developing.

We use images in our information packs and web-based presentations. We believe a picture can say so much more about an individual than just mere words. We want to use images of the target audience to reach out to them with our message – to engage them. We want them to think about changing their lifestyle.

Sun, UV and cancer

When the sun is strong, spend time in the shade, cover up with clothing and use sunscreen with at least SPF 15 and 4 stars.

Overexposure to ultraviolet (UV) light from the sun or sunbeds is the main cause of skin cancer.

YOU CAN **BE SMOKE FREE**

CANCER RESEARCH UK

We know lifestyle can affect already present conditions by causing genetic faults in cells that can go on to develop cancer over time. We want to make that link explicit – that repeated activities within a lifestyle can contribute directly to causing cancer. We want to produce visuals that show how this happens – a timeline that shows people how the disease can develop – to encourage them to recognise where they are on the timeline and make changes.

We know some activities have been shown to link directly to certain cancers – research has proved the link between smoking and lung cancer, and that over exposure to the sun and UV rays can cause skin cancer. An unhealthy lifestyle, eating too much and not exercising can also raise the risk of developing cancers. We want to produce imagery that will tackle these lifestyle choices and their dangers head on.

We want to use visuals to make our information packs and web materials hit home, giving messages such as four out of ten cancers could be avoided by lifestyle changes; smoking doesn't just cause lung cancer – it's linked to around a dozen other cancers, accounting for around 20% of all cancers in the UK; smoking, poor diet, alcohol and excess weight cause more than 120,000 cases of cancer each year in the UK.

We want to support our volunteers and recognise their importance to us. We are considering ideas such as uniforms – these ideas might be sweats that have a message relating to lifestyle; when thinking uniform, we want designers to think as creatively about this as possible.

More information: www.cancerresearchuk.org

Cancer Research UK Big Issues

Generating income to support cancer research through fundraising

Fundraising is vital to us. We know that our work makes a difference. For instance, we have contributed to work in radiotherapy that has improved recovery rates – four in ten people who beat cancer have received radiotherapy as part of their treatment, and we support more than 250 clinical trials across the UK. We manage these through our fundraising efforts.

We fund over 4000 doctors and nurses in the UK. We want to use visuals that show and communicate the importance of these people in developing care and support for patients.

The drugs we use to treat cancer cost money. We can't get around this. Trials and laboratory testing also cost money. We work with pharmaceutical companies to try and fast track the development of new drugs. To do this we need to invest money in our programmes. We want to promote our work through targeted advertising. We want to develop a strategy where our work is seen by as wide a range of people as possible, and to use persuasive language alongside imagery to gain their support for our fundraising.

We are finding new ways for people to work with us, such as our Citizen Science projects – these include Cell Slider and our mobile game 'Play to Cure: Genes in Space', which allow anyone to help analyse scientific data. These ideas will involve more people in our work, and we want to encourage this through visuals that promote our identity.

We need to continue to generate income through fundraising. We do this by supporting a network of volunteers, who then support our work through organising events. We want to include young people and young adults in our volunteer group as their work will relate to the target audience.

We use money to change people's approaches to cancer – early diagnosis and self-awareness can be vital in preventing the disease developing fully. We want to bring about a major shift in early diagnosis research, by investing £20 million each year by 2019.

For more information about Cancer Research UK go to www.cancerresearchuk.org.

Responding to the brief

When **reading** and **responding** to a brief that requires you to produce a presentation for a client that demonstrates your ideas in response to a brief, consider the **requirements of the brief**.

1   Read the **revision task brief** on pages 87–88. Underline key phrases and summarise the key points below.

....

....

....

....

....

....

....

....

....

....

....

....

2   Read the **revision task information** on pages 89–91. Underline key phrases and summarise the key points below.

....

....

....

....

....

....

....

....

....

....

....

....

....

3 Read the client information on pages 92–98 and complete the notes below.

(a) Client: Cancer Research UK – consider:

- history and culture, products and services, customers and market

- current designs and use of media such as websites and advertising

- legal, ethical and any environmental factors that apply.

(b) Purpose: what does the client wish to achieve?

- Increase participation and support of two target groups in its 'big issues'.

- ....

....

- ....

....

(c) Audience: who are the target groups and what are the considerations?

- Age: 11–18 or ....

- ....

....

- ....

....

(d) Outcome: what are the outcomes and how will they be produced?

- Develop a distinct identity for its visual materials and staff (e.g. literature, visual information, uniforms, props, marketing materials (physical/web based), interactive app for instant fundraising).

- ....

....

- ....

....

4 Note the choices you would make as an initial response to the brief, bearing in mind research and ideas generation.

Choice of **one target audience** age: ....

Choice of **one big issue** from the three options: ....

Choice of **one client brief** reflecting my art and design discipline: ....

Choice of **one** from three **options** within my art and design discipline brief: ....

> **Links** To revise understanding a brief, see page 96 of the Revision Guide.

Managing your time and records

An important part of managing a client brief is considering project management influences, such as timetabling, resources available and recording your research and preparation.

Ask your tutor or check the up-to-date Sample Assessment Material on the Pearson website to find out how many hours you have for research and preparation in your actual assessment. You do not need to complete the Revision Workbook activities in the same time, but make sure you know how to manage and complete the work within the allocated time in your assessment.

1 List all the things you will need to do in your research and preparation. Consider how you will manage your time to achieve this. Start with reading through the brief and end with all your research and preparation ready for producing the presentation. Use a format of choice to plan and track your time, for example a Gantt chart.

Make sure you leave time for reflection and to accommodate any unforeseen problems. You may find you need to update your timetable if things take more or less time than you plan.

Managing research and preparation time

◆ Guided

2 Complete the mind map below that considers ways to manage and organise the records of your research and preparation in a way that is relevant and useful when you produce and justify your presentation of ideas.

Record your research visually and in written format to demonstrate the full process you move through.

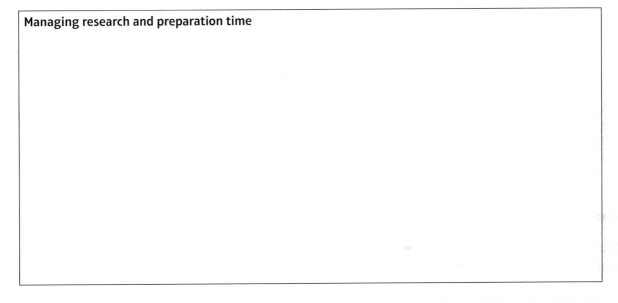

Headings to keep research in order

Drawing techniques, e.g. of processes, set-ups and visualising ideas

Annotation, to critically analyse work, noting ideas and planning future ideas

Organising research

Recording research findings

Using recording techniques

Links
To revise managing time, see page 96 of the Revision Guide, and to revise recording your research, see page 105 of the Revision Guide.

Planning your response

The plan you make in response to a brief is key in identifying how you will select and address the big issue, client's requirements and audience needs.

> When you have identified which **big issue** and **target audience** you will address, use the activities below to note your initial thoughts about links between them and any opportunities and challenges these might present. You could relate this to the Cancer Research UK brief or a brief for another organisation you have researched.

Guided

1 Define the characteristics of the target audience and how these characteristics might be used to engage with this big issue.

My selected target audience is ....

Characteristics of this target audience might include ....

I can use these characteristics to engage them with this big issue by ....

....

....

2 List **four** ways you could carry out research to address this issue and engage the audience.

> For example, you might wish to research the way technical information about cancer is currently communicated. You might need to think about different ways of communicating it to your target audience. You could consider the potential of visuals to communicate information. This could be educational, but if related to lifestyle choices could also be used to drive home a message.

Big issue: ....

Four ways to carry out research to address this issue and engage the audience:

1 ....

2 ....

3 ....

4 ....

Guided

3 Complete the mind map below with some initial planning.

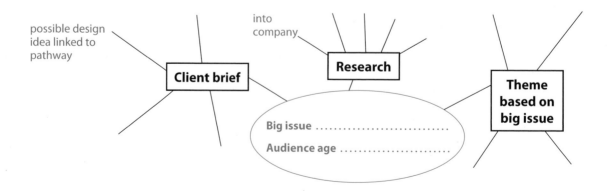

 Links To revise the client, audience and outcome, see page 97 of the Revision Guide.

Understanding client requirements

Understanding the client is an important part of managing the brief and developing relevant design ideas.

> Complete the activities below to help with your understanding of the client's requirements. You could relate this to the Cancer Research UK brief or a brief for another organisation you have researched.

Guided

1   List **three** benefits or outcomes the client wants to achieve from the brief, beyond the big issues.

> This is about extracting information from the brief.

1   The client wants to encourage people to be more aware of the different types of cancer.

2   ....

3   ....

2   How would you define the personality of the client as a charity?

> Consider how the client presents themselves in their branding and house style, including any requirements in relation to size, materials and sustainability, for example. Explore words to help define the personality of the client, for example professional, innovative, traditional, conservative, respected, approachable, caring.

....

....

....

....

Guided

3   Summarise the brief in your own words based on the audience you have selected, the big issue you are focusing on and your initial ideas in response. The brief gives links to information useful for research.

> Consider what personality the product has to represent and the client's specific requirements. Take into account constraints, for example time, budget, personal skills, resources and access. Keep a record of your ideas.

Key information about the client's history, identity,

products and services, branding, colours, style,

and purpose of brief, include: ....

....

....

The audience and their characteristics include: ....

The big issue for this brief is ....

The product for this brief could be ....

....

....

....

Links   To revise producing initial ideas and analysing client information, see pages 98–100 of the Revision Guide.

Researching audience needs

Your response to the revision brief must involve research so that you understand how to meet the audience needs. You need to select relevant information and material to inform and develop design ideas.

> Complete the activities below to help with your research into audience needs. You could relate this to the Cancer Research UK brief or a brief for another organisation you have researched.

Guided

1 Describe **three** methods you can use to find out information about your selected target audience.

> This might involve both academic and practical research and will depend on the target audience you select. List anything you can easily experience and access to start the research. Consider **primary research**, e.g. interviews, surveys, questionnaires, focus groups and **secondary research**, e.g. data shown to be important by the client or from other research sources. Identify gaps in information during research and respond to them.

> Think about ways to find out your audience's understanding of the organisation and to test out ways that you could increase awareness of a service. It will be important to record your research in different ways, for example record interviews (with permission), create a survey, draw and sketch, photograph, and so on.

   1   I could do some market research by interviewing people who work with my client who might be able to help with factual information. I can then relate this to my questions to my target audience.

   2   ....

   3   ....

Guided

2 Select **three** key characteristics you believe will be important to consider when designing for this target group, briefly explaining why.

> Think about the audience's demographics, for example age, gender, socio-economic groups, geographical location, ethnic, cultural and religious background, and income. Consider the context of the audience and any other products and services your design will be competing with to attract the audience's attention.

   1   The use of images in a recognisable brand is important to this group as it helps them relate to an organisation's personality and products or services, and this group responds to visual cues.

   2   ....

   3   ....

3 Sum up in one statement how you think you can respond to the brief, considering the audience's needs and the potential in the specific client brief you have selected.

....

....

....

....

....

> **Links** To revise analysing the audience, see pages 97 and 101 of the Revision Guide.

Analysing audience needs

To investigate ways of developing a design solution that is creative and functional it is useful to analyse how audience needs are currently met.

> Complete the activities below to help with your analysis of audience needs. You could relate this to the Cancer Research UK brief or a brief for another organisation you have researched.
>
> Analyse the experience of the target audience with different kinds of products that may take an inventive approach to learning. How do they engage the target audience, and how might this inform your own thinking?

1 Choose some organisations that work in the same field as your client.

....

....

....

....

....

Guided **2** Describe **three** ways you can measure how they meet their audience's needs.

> You will need to apply research techniques to find meaningful data.

1   I could source data on the amount of funds other ....

2   ....

3   ....

3 Reflect on these organisations and how well they seem to perform in meeting the target audience's needs when compared to your client. Select **one** to analyse in more detail.

> When assessing how organisations in a similar sector engage with your target audience, start by identifying approaches that seem stronger or weaker. Evaluate why you think this, and how they are different or similar. Where approaches taken seem stronger with the target audience than your client's approaches, consider how your ideas can be informed by this knowledge.

....

....

....

....

....

....

....

....

Links To revise analysing the audience, see pages 97–101 of the Revision Guide.

Connecting with the audience

When you have considered audience needs in relation to the brief, you would need to test out some points from your analysis to explore whether they could be used as starting points for initial ideas.

> Complete the activities below to test out your findings. You could relate this to the Cancer Research UK brief or a brief for another organisation you have researched.

Guided

1 Start by describing **four** ways the organisation currently achieves connection with the chosen target audience.

> These can be based on your initial analysis of the brief or from some new research.

1 The organisation is proactive in seeking solutions to ....

2 The organisation expects its audience to be comfortable using technology to support learning

   – they provide a lot of online support material ....

3 ....

4 ....

2 From your research, select the **two** most important ways the organisation could connect with the target audience you have chosen, and explain why you have selected these ways.

> In your explanation, make clear references to the client, the target audience and your research.

1 ....

....

....

....

....

....

2 ....

....

....

....

....

....

Links To revise analysing the audience, see page 101 of the Revision Guide.

Visual requirements and constraints

You need to identify requirements and constraints of the client brief and apply them when planning and managing your response to the brief.

> Complete the activities below to establish requirements and constraints. You could relate this to the Cancer Research UK brief or a brief for another organisation you have researched.

Guided   **1**   Complete the mind map below to revise the key visual information you need to apply when developing your response to this brief. Add further requirements or constraints you consider important.

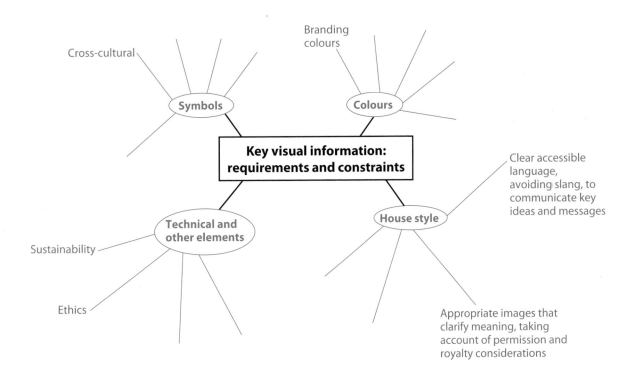

2   Select the **two** pieces of visual information you think are the most important in meeting this brief. On the next page, explain why you think they are the most important.

> You need to link audience and client needs with the pieces of visual information you think are most important for your chosen art and design pathway and brief.
>
> Consider:
> - how your two pieces of visual information might impact on the potential design
> - whether the issues compete against each other with a potentially negative impact or whether they easily tie together for incorporating into one art and design message or outcome
> - the common considerations of your specialism, for example:
>   - **3D design**: strength, safety, durability, sustainability, finish, balance, weight
>   - **fashion**: sizes, washing, cost, sustainability, allergy, equality and diversity
>   - **textiles**: safety, durability, sustainability, hanging, presentation, hand-made or manufactured
>   - **photography**: ethics, privacy, copyright, format, empathy, resolution, colour mode, printed/screen
>   - **fine art**: scale, weight, safety, material, durability, product application
>   - **graphics**: colour mode, resolution, copyright, stock vector or raster, accessibility
>   - **interactive design**: compatibility, file type, platform, audience ability.
>
> Consider how the requirements and constraints relate to the client's personality and activities and how the client wants to come across.

1 ....

....

....

....

....

....

....

....

....

....

....

....

2 ....

....

....

....

....

....

....

....

....

....

....

....

Links To revise analysis, research, and working with requirements and constraints, see pages 102–105 of the Revision Guide.

Generating and selecting ideas

When you have a full understanding of the brief and your research, you need to generate and select ideas.

Complete the activities below to generate ideas in response to a client brief. You could relate this to the Cancer Research UK brief or a brief for another organisation you have researched.

1 Generate **two** ideas based on your initial research and ideas. Start by listing your selected big issue, target audience and client brief.

Refer to all these factors in your work.

1 Big issue ....

2 Target audience ....

3 Client brief ....

Guided

2 Summarise how you feel Idea 1 will meet the client and audience requirements in the brief and provide annotated diagrams/sketches below.

> Any combination of text, image, drawing and annotation is a good approach, as long as it clearly takes into account your research and shows your ideas. Keep a record of your work and decisions, for example ways that you tested out your ideas, costs involved and resources needed, as they will help inform the presentation of your ideas.
> • Make sure your annotations of sketches and drawings include key words.
> • Think about the language and terminology you use, including key words, when describing the ideas.
> • Explain your choice of formal elements and materials, techniques and processes.
> • Note any resources you will need to complete your idea and be sure you can access them.

Idea 1 meets the client requirements because ....

....

This idea meets the audience requirements because ....

....

Idea 1

Links To revise ideas generation and selection, see pages 106–112 of the Revision Guide. To revise formal elements, materials, techniques and processes, see pages 12–13 in Unit 1 of this Revision Workbook.

> **Guided**

3 Summarise how you feel Idea 2 will meet the audience and client requirements in the brief and provide annotated diagrams/sketches below.

Idea 2 meets the client requirements because ....

....

....

This idea meets the audience requirements because ....

....

....

Idea 2

> **Guided**

4 Select the idea that you think will best meet the audience and client requirements in the brief and explain why.

> Consider why it best meets the needs, purpose and requirements of the brief. Show why it is relevant to the needs of the audience and client. Explain how it responds to your research findings and testing out of the designs on the target audience. Be sure you can access all the resources you need to take the idea forward.

Idea .... best meets the client and audience requirements because ....

....

....

....

Refining and justifying an idea

You will need to select one idea to take forward as the most appropriate to address the brief in the revision task.

Complete the activities below to consider ways of refining and justifying ideas in response to a client brief. You could relate this to the Cancer Research UK brief or a brief for another organisation you have researched.

Guided **1** Use the diagram below to help clarify your intentions about the idea you wish to take forward.

A diagram can help you to visualise all the points and how they relate. It can also help you to review your concepts and use of formal elements, materials, techniques and processes, and make any refinements to your idea.

How it meets client's requirements:
- Relates to statements of intention in client brief, to do with the big issue
- ....
  ....
  ....
- ....
  ....
  ....

Selected client brief:
....

Selected idea
....

Proposed outcome in response to the brief:
....

How it meets audience's needs:
- They will be able to see the benefits of
  ....
- ....
  ....
  ....
- ....
  ....

Guided **2** Complete the mind map below with factors you could evaluate against when refining and improving your ideas and justifying your choices.

Using visuals and annotations can help demonstrate the development process and be useful in your presentation. Note that the brief on page 87 states that the idea you include in your presentation does not have to be a fully finished design.

Contextual analysis – cover client and audience needs, and purpose of the brief

Compare different design approaches – show amendments and annotate with the reason why

Refining ideas

 Links To revise selecting, justifying and refining ideas, see pages 109–112 of the Revision Guide.

Reviewing the development process

Taking an overview of your response to the brief will allow you to make accurate judgements about how it meets audience and client needs, and help inform the structure and content of your presentation.

> Complete the activities below to review the development process overall in preparation for your presentation in response to a client brief. You could relate this to the Cancer Research UK brief or a brief for another organisation you have researched.

1 Write a summary of your response to the client brief. Explain how you worked on each stage and how your ideas progressed. Think about the way you used research, and any contextual influences.

....

....

....

....

2 Critically reflect on your choice of final idea for the client brief, below. (For example, how many initial ideas did you come up with? What influenced you to choose the final one?)

> Being honest in your critical reflection is important. Acknowledging decisions that didn't work well shows that you can review your own work dispassionately. You can also compare and contrast to show how this process led to better decisions, and might inform different decisions in future.

   (a)   Selection criteria – what did you consider when selecting the final idea?

....

....

....

   (b)   Audience needs – how does the final idea meet these?

....

....

....

   (c)   Client requirements – how does the final idea meet these?

....

....

....

   (d)   Creative intention – did the final idea meet your own creative expectations?

....

....

....

> Your choices should relate to the client's brief.

3 It is important to justify your response to the brief. Addressing the key points below will help inform your presentation slides and speaker notes. Include relevant information on any important choices you made while developing your idea.

> Justifying your selection and choices is a key aspect of your presentation. Consider what you are trying to get across and use appropriate language and terminology when writing your justifications.

(a) Your choice of formal elements, materials, techniques and processes ....

....

....

....

(b) How your ideas address your target audience ....

....

....

....

....

(c) How your ideas address the big issue you selected ....

....

....

....

....

(d) How your ideas met the client brief ....

....

....

....

....

....

Presenting a response to a client brief

When presenting a response to a client brief, you will need to use an appropriate format and method of presentation. The revision brief on page 87 requests a presentation with no more than 20 slides.

> Complete the activities below to consider ways of organising information and practical outcomes for the presentation in response to a client brief. You could relate this to the Cancer Research UK brief or a brief for another organisation you have researched.

Guided

1 List **five** factors that may determine how you select imagery for your slides.

> Think about how the visuals explain your progress and response throughout the brief.

  1 Shows the way key visual information was incorporated.

  2 ....

  3 ....

  4 ....

  5 ....

2 Take **one** of the above factors and describe how you might arrange visual and textual information on a slide to show this. Keep the layout of the slide in mind as you place the visuals. You can plan your layout using the space below.

> You can use visuals to support your explanations. Make sure they are selected to be relevant, are produced in high quality and are well presented.

3 Taking your response to question 2, write some single words or short phrases that could be included on an actual slide to reinforce your intention.

> Fewer words on a slide work better than many words. Text should enhance or explain the visual material but not repeat it.

  ....

  ....

  ....

> **Links** To revise presenting a response to a client brief, see pages 113–125 of the Revision Guide.

Guided 4 Look at the slide below and on page 116. One is an effective slide and one is a weaker example. List at least **four** reasons that make each slide either effective or weak, and explain why. You can annotate the slide and use circles and arrows to highlight specific visuals and identify your points.

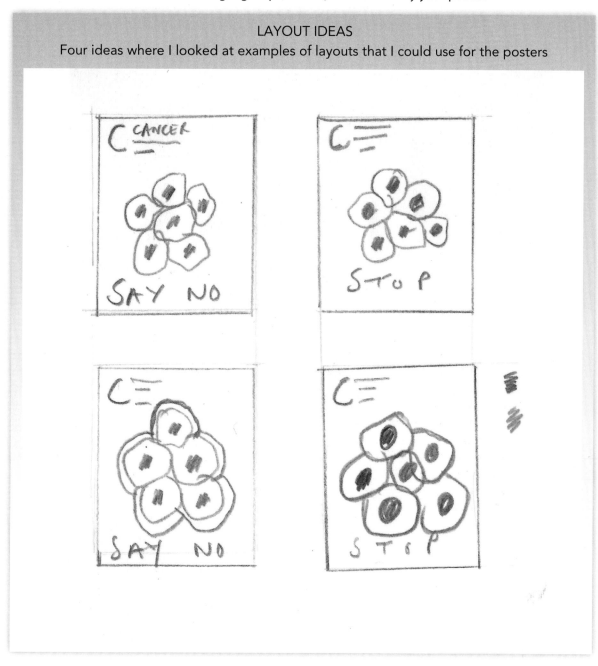

LAYOUT IDEAS
Four ideas where I looked at examples of layouts that I could use for the posters

I think this slide is stronger/weaker than the slide on page 116 for the following reasons:

1 ....

2 ....

3 ....

4 ....

5   Now list **four** reasons that make this slide more effective or weaker than the slide on page 115 and explain why. You can annotate the slide and use circles and arrows to highlight specific visuals and identify your points.

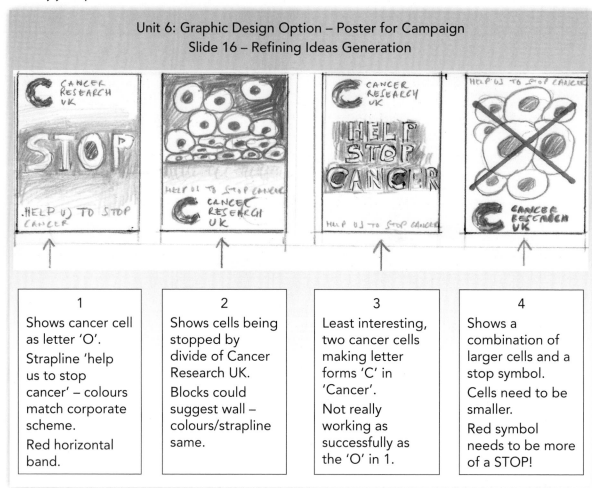

I think this slide is stronger/weaker than the slide on page 115 for the following reasons:

1   ....

2   ....

3   ....

4   ....

6 Now you have identified what makes slides effective, use the ideas from the examples to show how you would construct your own final slide of the presentation. Consider carefully how you will use the final slide to present and explain the idea to be taken forward.

> Each slide in your presentation should be **relevant** and **concise**. Consider:
> - the number of the slide in the sequence of no more than 20 slides and the job it is doing
> - the heading you will use to show the focus of the slide
> - how you will use the slide to show the effective development of that stage of your ideas
> - how you will choose and use relevant visuals to clearly show the development process
> - how you will use key annotations/labels/text to support your explanation – use only small amounts of text so that the points are clear and can be read easily.
>
> You can use grid lines to help you position items in the slide. For your actual assessment, make sure you are familiar with the software you will be using.

 Links To revise presenting a response to a client brief, see pages 113–125 of the Revision Guide.

Planning a professional presentation

You will need to structure your presentation so that it presents the development of your idea, using relevant text and visuals. Make sure that you position important concepts and images in places that have impact. You will also need to prepare speaker notes (see page 121).

 Complete the activities below to consider the best ways of sequencing your presentation. You could relate this to the Cancer Research UK brief or a brief for another organisation you have researched.

You will need to plan to:

- organise information and practical outcomes
- produce and finalise visual parts of the presentation
- introduce and frame the concept
- present ideas with supporting explanations, showing how your ideas meet the brief
- demonstrate how each aspect of the client brief has been addressed, making links between the client requirements and your ideas
- justify decisions and design choices
- consider appropriateness for audience
- summarise and conclude.

1 Use the list of words below to help draft the order of a client presentation, using no more than 20 slides in total. You can:
- add words to those suggested
- put more than one topic on one slide
- use more than one slide to cover one topic
- indicate the selection of visuals and accompanying text that might go on each slide.

> Think about the running order and how the slides will communicate your journey through your response to the brief. You are describing what the slides should contain and in which order they go. You could sketch in images or frames for where photos might go. Number the slides so you know what order they come in. Use a pencil so that you can easily make adjustments.

Client, brief, target audience, initial ideas, visual sources, contextual research, selecting ideas, testing and feedback, addressing the big issues, developing, constraints, visual, unique, response, art and design outcome, research, overview, formal elements, materials, techniques, processes

1

2

Continue to plan the slide presentation about your journey through the brief using the ideas on page 118.

3

4

5

6

7

8

9

10

11

12

Continue to plan the slide presentation about your journey through the brief using the ideas on page 118. For Slide 20, refer to your work on page 117 for how you will present and explain the final art and design idea to be taken forward, and how it successfully answers the client's brief.

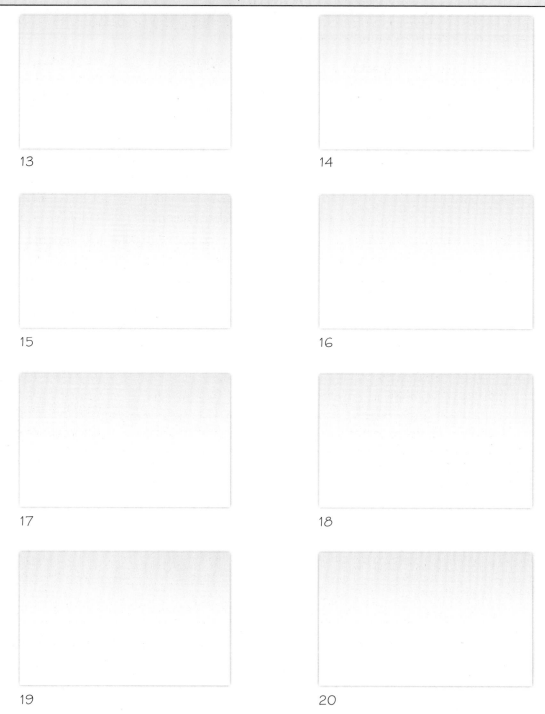

13

14

15

16

17

18

19

20

2 Review your draft presentation with reference to the brief. If needed, revise the slide plan to adjust it or add more detail. Make sure you are using no more than 20 slides in total and that:

Consider the order of the slides, and change it if needed.

- important images or photos are indicated
- the important content is covered within the slides
- you put the three most important slides of the presentation in important places.

 Links To revise effective presentations in response to a client brief, see pages 113–125 of the Revision Guide.

Presenting ideas with explanations

You will need to clearly explain the development of your ideas and how they meet the brief in your presentation. If producing a slide show of no more than 20 slides, your **speaker notes** will support any visuals, annotations and notes on your slides.

Guided > **1** List **four** things your speaker notes might contain and communicate.

> Use concise speaker notes to emphasise points that you can't get across in depth on the slides.

(a) Reinforcing the point about how a design idea uses brand colours to meet client requirements

(b) ....

(c) ....

(d) ....

2 Summarising information is important when writing speaker notes. The following text is taken from a sketchbook that related to one aspect of a client brief. Summarise the following text into brief bullet-point notes that can be used as support for writing speaker notes.

> When making notes, pull out only the important points, making them brief but accurate.

> I tried really hard to come up with a new layout idea but I've been stuck, finally got something just by playing around with the visuals in software, printing them out and drawing into them, don't know if this is going to work as I don't think it's the most exciting idea. Still stuck, can't see how I'm going to get the idea of the organisation across without spelling it out, plus my ideas for layout are really not happening – need to get more information maybe? Not enjoying this at moment.
>
> Really positive news – found an example of layout for the organisation that finally inspired me, am able to see how the text and imagery (it's like small molecules) could be used to get across the importance of the scientific work they do. Can see now how this can be developed to even go as far as being used in a logo and corporate literature/design – need to work out how layout and colour best work now, but have an area to work within.

Summary notes

- ....

....

....

....

....

....

....

....

....

Links To revise writing supportive notes in response to a client brief, see page 126 of the Revision Guide.

3 Produce an outline of what would be important in speaker notes for the final slide of your presentation. Look at the ideas on pages 117–120 to help you outline your response to the brief and how the research and development of ideas addresses the client and audience needs.

When bringing the presentation to a conclusion, it should:

- address the most important issues with reasoned argument
- promote your product
- have impact on your clients
- end in a short and memorable way and leave your clients feeling positive.

> When writing speaker notes, consider different ways of making them brief and easy to read. For example:
> - write in note form, not continuous prose
> - use titles, headings and bullet points
> - explain and provide information on the contents of each slide
> - highlight any key points or aspects of your work the slide shows
> - make it very clear how you have refined your work and the reasoning behind this
> - make sure you use the correct terminology and use the spellchecker so your work is accurate.

Speaker notes: Slide no: ....

- ....

....

....

....

....

....

....

....

....

....

....

....

....

....

....

....

....

....

Links To revise writing supportive notes in response to a client brief, see pages 126–127 of the Revision Guide.

Revision activity

Ask your tutor or look at the Sample Assessment Materials on the Pearson website to find out how long you have for your assessed activity in your actual assessment and whether you can take in work from the research and preparatory stage. Make sure you plan your time so that you can complete your activity in the allocated time.

Although the revision brief includes researching and producing a presentation to increase participation and support for Cancer Research UK, the activities in this Workbook will only require you to focus on the skills associated with this activity. You are **not** expected to undertake full research, preparation and production of a presentation. Although the brief and associated tasks are specific to Cancer Research UK, the activities in this Workbook also allow you to demonstrate your skills in a wider context.

Revision activity 1

Produce a presentation for the client that demonstrates your ideas in response to a client brief.

Consider how you will include in your presentation:

- the target audience and big issue you have chosen to respond to
- how you have selected and used the information from the client pack to inform your ideas
- how you developed your ideas from the initial stages through to the final idea
- your final idea in response to **one** of the client briefs
- visual representation of your ideas
- your choice of formal elements and materials, techniques and processes
- how your ideas address the target audience you have selected
- how your ideas address the big issue you have selected
- justification of how your ideas meet the client brief.

The presentation should contain no more than 20 slides with accompanying speaker notes.

 Prepare a short slide presentation of research and work you have completed to meet a brief. You could use work completed in relation to Cancer Research UK or another organisation.

Include:

- an opening slide

- a slide that visually shows key development of ideas in relation to the audience needs

- a concluding slide.

If possible, prepare the presentation using the software and equipment you will use in your actual assessment.

Unit 7: Developing and Realising Creative Intentions

Your set task

Unit 7 will be assessed through a task, which will be set by Pearson. You will research, develop and produce a proposal and a piece of art and design with a clear purpose in a discipline of your choice, in response to a given theme. You will also provide supporting written material at the end of the process.

Your Revision Workbook

This Workbook is designed to **revise skills** that you might need in your assessed task. The selected content, outcomes, questions and answers are provided to help you to revise content and ways of applying your skills. Ask your tutor or check the **Pearson website** for the most up-to-date **Sample Assessment Material** and **Mark Scheme** to get an indication of the structure of your actual assessed task and what this requires of you. Pay attention to requirements in relation to submission of images and portfolio, whether you have access to a computer, which activities are unsupervised or supervised, allocation of time and whether you can take any research and preparatory work into the supervised assessment. The details of the actual assessed task may change so always make sure you are up to date.

1 Research and develop initial ideas in response to a theme (pages 133–144)

- **Read** and **respond** to starting points on a specified theme that would result in a piece of art and design in a discipline of your choice that has a clear purpose.
- **Revise** the **skills** needed to produce an annotated log of research and preparatory explorations into trends, contextual factors and artists/designers relevant to a theme and the development of your ideas in response, including samples, mock-ups and written notes on your decisions and refinements.

2 Prepare to produce a proposal explaining how you intend to respond to a theme (pages 145–147)

Revise the skills needed to propose your art and design piece, including details on: initial ideas for the focus of the piece which must have a clear purpose and reasons for your choice; the research plan into contextual sources and trends; the materials, techniques and processes you want to use; your plan to complete the work within time; identification of equipment and specialist expertise that may be required.

3 Consider a piece of art and design in response to a theme (pages 148–156)

The art and design piece must have a clear purpose for which you would produce a proposal, and the idea would be realised into a fully developed piece of art and design in a discipline of your choice.

4 Consider production of a digital portfolio (pages 157–160)

Revise the skills needed to: demonstrate your development and realisation process in a digital portfolio of between 16 and 20 pages, where each page can include a combination of images and written work; select key pieces of your development work to include with supporting written annotations explaining the development process, and select and produce images of your final art and design piece.

5 Prepare to produce a commentary (pages 161–163)

Revise the skills for producing a commentary of your development and realisation process to accompany each page of the digital portfolio. The commentary should include explanations of the development processes, how you achieved your final piece, how it responds to the theme, and it should evaluate the development process and the final piece.

6 Respond to activities (pages 164–166)

Revise the skills involved when producing a proposal explaining how you intend to respond to a theme, and producing a commentary to accompany the digital portfolio.

Links To help you revise skills that might be needed in your Unit 7 assessed task this Workbook contains a revision task starting on page 125. Activities to help you develop the skills needed for your task begin on page 131. The introduction on page iii has more information on revision features.

Revision task

To support your revision, this Workbook contains a revision task to help you **revise the skills** that you might need in your assessed task. Ask your tutor or check the Pearson website for the most up-to-date **Sample Assessment Material** and **Mark Scheme** to get an idea of of the structure of the actual assessed task and what this requires of you. The details of the actual assessed task may change so always make sure you are up to date.

Revision task brief

Although you are given a revision brief that includes researching, developing and realising creative intentions in response to a brief for a piece of art and design that has a clear purpose with a theme of 'Structure', the activities in this Workbook will only require you to focus on the skills associated with the tasks. You are **not** expected to undertake full research, development and production of a piece of art and design nor associated tasks such as a full proposal, portfolio and commentary. Although the theme in the revision brief is 'Structure', the activities in this Workbook may also involve a wider range of images to demonstrate skills that you can apply with any theme.

Start by reading the brief below.

For this task you will produce a piece of art and design work that responds to the theme 'Structure'.

A document is provided on pages 129–130 with a series of images, quotations, artists and designers that will provide starting points for the development of your ideas.

The art and design piece you produce can be in an art and design discipline of your choice and must have a clear purpose.

For example:
- a piece of artwork for an exhibition
- advertising or promotional material
- interactive product
- commercial design/product
- functional object
- fashion garment or accessory.

You will demonstrate the development and realisation of your art and design piece by producing an art and design portfolio.

Your portfolio will contain a selection of the drafts, samples and mock-ups of the developing work, evidence of your research into trends, contextual factors and artists and/or designers, and images of your final art and design piece. This will be accompanied by a written commentary of the development and realisation process.

In this task you will demonstrate how you are able to:
- develop a specific art and design idea against a theme for a clear purpose for which you will produce a proposal
- realise your idea into a fully developed piece of art and design
- demonstrate the design and realisation of the work through a digital portfolio and an evaluative record.

Revision activities

Although the revision task refers to researching, developing and realising creative intentions in response to a brief for a piece of art and design that has a clear purpose with a theme of 'Structure', the activities in this Workbook will only require you to focus on the skills associated with the tasks. You are **not** expected to undertake full research, development and production of a piece of art and design nor associated tasks such as a full proposal, portfolio and commentary. Although the theme in the revision brief is 'Structure', the activities in this Workbook may also involve a wider range of images to demonstrate skills that you can apply with any theme. Ask your tutor or check the up-to-date Sample Assessment Material on the Pearson website to get an indication of the structure of your actual assessed task and what this requires of you. Pay attention to which activities are unsupervised or supervised, and the time allowed. The details of the actual assessed task may change so always make sure you are up to date.

Revision activity 1

Research and development of initial ideas.

You must carry out significant research and preparatory explorations before beginning your art and design piece.

You must keep an annotated log of the research you carried out and the development of your ideas. This will ensure you have materials to select for your digital portfolio. The log should include samples and mock-ups of your work, evidence of your research into trends, contextual factors and artists and/ or designers who inspire you. You must also keep written notes on your decisions and your refinements throughout the process.

Revision activity 2

Produce a proposal explaining how you intend to respond to the theme.

The proposal must include details on:
- your initial ideas for the focus of your art and design piece
- the reasons for your choice of art and design piece
- your research plan into contextual sources and trends
- your initial ideas on the materials, techniques and processes you want to use
- your plans to complete the work within the time
- identification of the equipment and specialist expertise you may require.

Make sure you demonstrate your skills in:
- explanation of ideas in relation to the theme
- selection of research sources
- explanation of the materials, techniques and processes you intend to use.

Revision activity 3

Produce a piece of art and design in a discipline of your choice and with a clear purpose.

Revision activity 4

Produce a digital portfolio that demonstrates your development and realisation process.

Photograph or scan selected pieces of development work and the final piece to include in your digital portfolio.

- Consideration should be given to the quality of the images selected for the portfolio. These should be of sufficient size to show the quality of the work.
- Work that is intended to be accessed digitally should be submitted as PDF documents.
- 3D and larger pieces must be photographed and include an indication of scale. No more than four photographs are allowed per piece (one image of the work in its entirety and three further images of different angles and/or details).

You must produce between 16 and 20 pages for your digital portfolio.

Each page can include a combination of images and written work.

You must:

- select key pieces of your development work to include in your digital portfolio
- select images of your final art and design piece
- produce supporting written annotations explaining your development process
- produce images of your final art and design piece.

Make sure you demonstrate your skills in:

- your creative response to the theme
- the use of contextual sources and influences in your work
- your exploration of materials, techniques and processes in your development work
- your ability to refine your work through review and evaluation
- how well your portfolio shows the development and realisation processes
- the quality of presentation of the portfolio.

Revision activity 5

Produce a commentary of your development and realisation process to accompany each page of your digital portfolio.

This should include:

- explanations of your development processes
- explanations of how you achieved your final piece and how it responds to the theme
- an evaluation of the development process and the final piece of work.

Make sure you demonstrate your skills in:

- the quality and clarity of your explanation
- accurate use of spelling, grammar and subject-specific terminology.

Revision task information

This revision task information is used as an example to show the skills you need. The content of a task will be different each year and the format may be different. Ask your tutor or check the latest Sample Assessment Material on the Pearson website for more details.

Briefing sheet

THEME

'STRUCTURE'

You will explore and investigate the theme 'STRUCTURE' to produce creative outcomes. The theme is a starting point from which to develop your ideas. It will form the basis of your design ideas and contextual research into artists/designers/trends/movements that may inspire your work.

This document (pages 129–130) provides you with a series of images, quotations, artists and designers that will provide starting points for the development of your ideas.

STRUCTURE

Noun

The way in which the parts of a system or object are arranged or organised, or a system arranged in this way.

Synonyms: network/architecture/formation/system/framework/construction/organisation/anatomy/order/morphology

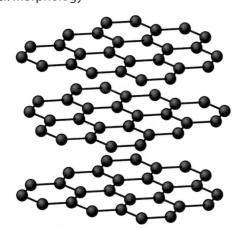

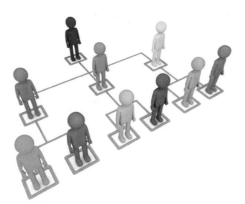

Management systems differ. Some have what might be seen as an old-fashioned management structure.

Quote 'Architecture depends on its time. It is the crystallization of its inner structure, the slow unfolding of its form.' Ludwig Mies van der Rohe

Source: 1950 Ludwig Mies van der Rohe: Technology and architecture (speech). In: Conrads, U. ed. *Programs and manifestoes on 20th-century architecture.* (1970). MIT Press, p154.

Mies van der Rohe, Vila Tugendhat, Brno, 1929–1930

ARTISTS AND DESIGNERS

Theo Jansen	Charles Eames
Daniel Libeskind	Vivienne Westwood
Andrea Zittel	Anish Kapoor
Gerhard Richter	Aardman Animations
Yinka Shonibare	Grayson Perry
Michael Brennand-Wood	Jenny Carlisle
Man Ray	Mies van der Rohe
Andy Goldsworthy	Brâncuși
Anthony Howe	Alexander Calder
Stefan Sagmeister	Zaha Hadid
Philippe Starck	Henri Matisse

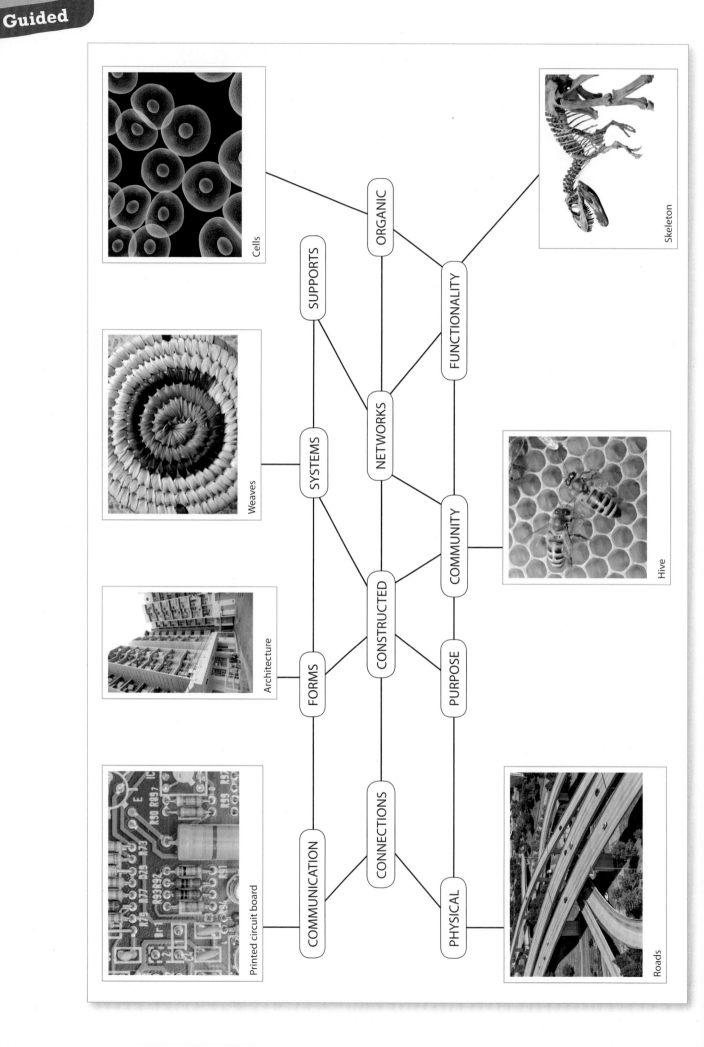

Cells

Skeleton

ORGANIC

SUPPORTS

FUNCTIONALITY

SYSTEMS

NETWORKS

Weaves

COMMUNITY

Hive

FORMS

CONSTRUCTED

Architecture

PURPOSE

COMMUNICATION

CONNECTIONS

PHYSICAL

Printed circuit board

Roads

Interpreting a brief

When **reading** and **responding** to a brief, consider the **requirements** of the brief.

1   Read the **revision task brief** on pages 125–127. Underline key phrases and summarise the key points below.

....

....

....

....

....

....

....

....

....

....

....

....

....

2   Read the **revision task information** on pages 128–130. Underline key phrases and summarise the key points below.

....

....

....

....

....

....

....

....

....

....

....

....

Check your understanding of key points, if taking forward the complete brief, against the points below. Tick the key points that you have noted on page 131. Then read through any additional points and tick them to show you understand what is required.

Research and prepare in response to a prescribed theme
- Respond to starting points on a theme that would result in a piece of art and design.
- Select a discipline of choice.
- Decide a clear purpose for the piece (for example, a piece of work for an exhibition, advertising or promotional material, interactive product, commercial design/product, functional object, fashion garment or accessory).
- Produce an annotated log of research and preparatory explorations.
- Research and explore trends, contextual factors, artists and/or designers relevant to a theme.
- Develop ideas in response to a theme, with samples, mock-ups and written notes.

Produce a proposal explaining how you intend to respond to a theme
- Explain initial ideas for the focus of the piece which must have a clear purpose.
- Explain the research and preparatory explorations plans.
- Explain the proposed materials, techniques and processes.
- Explain the plan to complete the scope of the work within timescales.
- Identify the equipment and specialist expertise that may be required.

Produce a piece of art and design in response to a theme
- Use a discipline of choice.
- Develop and realise a clear purpose for the piece.

Produce a digital portfolio
- Demonstrate the development and realisation process in 16–20 pages.
- Each page can combine images and written work.
- Select inclusion of key pieces of development work with explanatory written annotations.
- Select and produce images of the final art and design piece.

Produce a commentary
- Show your development and realisation process to accompany each page of the digital portfolio.
- Explain the development processes, how the final piece was achieved and how it responds to the theme.
- Evaluate the development process and the final piece.

> **Guided** 3 Note **three** key responses that you need to make to the brief.

    1 Respond to starting points on the theme of: ....

    2 Select a discipline of my choice: ....

    3 Decide a clear purpose: ....

Planning a response

When you have reflected on the brief and the theme, you need a plan to research and develop initial ideas. Your piece of art and design should be in your chosen discipline, with a clear purpose in response to the theme.

> Possible starting points can include work completed in past projects that may provide further exploration. Think creatively about how you can take forward ideas, knowledge and skills from the whole course.

Guided > **1** Consider at least **two** starting points for 'Structure' or another theme you choose. For example:

Forms found in organic structures like cells, rings in trees.

Your choices:

1 ....

2 ....

Guided > **2** Explain what attracted you to select each of these possible starting points. For example:

I'm interested in organic form and the complexity of forms in plants, cells and human form. I could use rings in trees to explore ideas about time, age and growth. The purpose is imagery for a TV trailer for a science series on conserving our planet as a living structure.

Your choices:

1 ....

....

2 ....

....

Guided > **3** Select **one** idea. List **two** example research sources for the idea (one primary and one secondary). For example:

Organic structures: primary source: actual examples of organic structures, locally or further afield; secondary source: scientific imagery of structures from science books or other practitioners.

Your choices:

....

....

4 Explain why the chosen idea offers the strongest potential as a starting point for your response.

....

....

> Keep a record of your research, development, decisions and refinements throughout the process. Written and visual work should be kept in an annotated log. This will provide information for your proposal, and sources/text/visuals to select for the digital portfolio and written commentary.

> 🔗 **Links** To revise starting points, see pages 129–130 of the Revision Guide.

Exploring and recording sources

As part of your research and development of initial ideas, you will need to explore and record your work. The exploration and records also inform the developed piece and provide material for the proposal and portfolio.

Complete the activities below to help with exploring and recording initial ideas. You could relate this to 'Structure' or another theme you are working with.

Guided 1 Create a mind map on research and recording below. Consider exploration of the idea, primary and secondary sources to use, and what techniques could be used to record. Include one source in direct relation to contemporary practice, trends or ideas in your specialist chosen pathway.

> Make sure your sources are realistic and accessible. Here is an example that has been started in relation to 'Structure.'
>
> Primary: plant-related forms, close-up drawings and photographs
>
> Primary: surfaces, brick, flooring, walls that co-exist with organic form – frottage
>
> **Structure: organic form**
>
> Primary and secondary: architecture incorporating organic form – drawings, photographs, internet
>
> Primary and secondary: growth/decay over time – time-lapse; photography; practitioner work (internet)

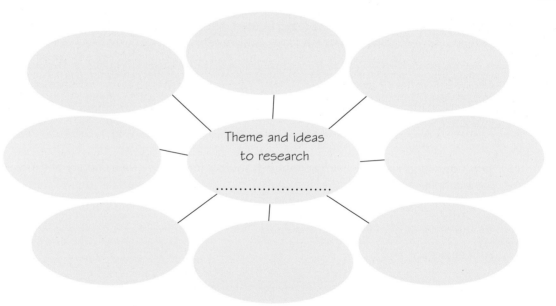

Theme and ideas
to research

....

2 Consider the source in direct relation to any contemporary practice, trends or ideas in your specialist chosen pathway. Explain how your initial thoughts on ideas and techniques are similar or different.

....

....

....

....

....

....

Links To revise exploration, sources and recording your work, see pages 131–133 of the Revision Guide.

Guided > **3** Using the mind map that you completed on page 134, select any **two** sources and the associated techniques that you feel would work best. Explain why.

Source 1 and associated recording technique ....

....

....

....

....

....

> Explanations can be pragmatic. For example:
> *Photography will work as I will have limited time so can't rely on drawing alone.*
>
> Explanations can also relate to specific techniques. Think about:
> • how techniques can work in recording a source such as frottage, photography, and drawing to record texture
> • why specific techniques are ideally suited to record specific sources – consider the visual appearance of a source and what elements it already shows, for example line, shape and so on.

Source 2 and associated recording technique ....

....

....

....

....

....

Guided > **4** Explain how formal elements and visual language might be recorded when working from these sources, using the associated techniques you have listed.

> **Links** Look at page 63 of this Revision Workbook to revise formal elements and visual language.

Source 1: recording formal elements and visual language ....

....

....

....

....

....

Source 2: recording formal elements and visual language ....

....

....

....

....

....

....

> **Links** To revise exploration, sources and recording your work, see pages 131–133 of the Revision Guide.

Generating ideas

Using the work you have done so far in researching a theme, generate two **initial ideas** that are informed by your mind map on page 134, relating to 'Structure' or another theme you are working with.

> In your actual assessment, you will need to keep an annotated log of the research and development of your ideas to ensure you have visual and written materials to select for your digital portfolio and written commentary. Your work in generating ideas will also inform your proposal and developed piece.

> **Guided**

1 Select **two** initial ideas relating to 'Structure' or another theme you have worked with. Create notes to explain your ideas. For example:

- I'm going to design imagery for a TV trailer for a science series on structures in the natural world. I'm going to use source materials in organic form, to explore the potential for using still imagery as well as slow moving close-ups.

- I'm interested in ideas I've begun to research, where practitioners consider the world as a living organism rather than something we can just exploit endlessly. I've read some complex texts on 'Vibrant Matter', which references some of these ideas. It is basically about looking at natural forms as having their own energy and purpose, and not only seeing them from our human perspective.

- My ideas will aim to show (a) the intricate nature of these structures to refocus our attention and appreciation of them; (b) the visual complexity or range of different types, and (c) how our activities with commercialism and industrialisation can destroy them. Although this area is not new, it is valid and developing. People of my age try to tackle these issues.

Your ideas:

Idea 1

- ....

....

....

....

....

....

Idea 2

- ....

....

....

....

....

....

 Links To revise generating ideas, see page 134 of the Revision Guide.

Developing and recording ideas

When **developing** and **recording** your ideas, it is important to plan how you might work with an idea from research to production. Consider primary and secondary sources, contextual influences, recording techniques, references to practitioners and potential application or product for the final piece.

> In your actual assessment, you will keep an annotated log of your research and development of ideas. The plans you make will also inform your proposal, digital portfolio, written commentary and developed work.

Guided ▷

1 Read the explanation below as an example of one way you could work through an idea from research to production, in relation to the theme 'Structure'. You can use this example to inform your own writing that follows on the next page.

- <u>Initial ideas</u>: I am going to create an exciting visual trailer – up to 30 seconds long, based on organic forms and the danger our industrialisation poses, as a metaphor for the danger we pose to our own world.

- <u>Research plan</u>: I'm going to research Cornelia Parker, whose work has influenced me in the past, and whose treatment of spaces and structures that are disconnected really interests me – it's not an obvious type of structure. I'm also going to look at contemporary practice that explores the theme of structure, from sewing to installation. I will also review a wide number of trailers and programme introductions on this area and documentaries/science programmes, from both TV and web-based channels, to see how they have used formal elements and visual language to communicate. I will also research some aspects of writings on 'Vibrant Matter'.

- <u>Materials, techniques and processes</u>: I am going to use a mixture of photography, film, drawing and layering. I will really need to separate out the visual recording techniques into two areas – the first will record the structures so will require specialist lenses and lighting; the second will explore the damage caused by human activity.

- <u>Time plan</u>: I'm going to check I know how many hours and weeks are allowed, and then divide the work into weeks, using the following kinds of stages:
  - o initial ideas and research
  - o exploration, testing, review and refinement
  - o further research
  - o production and review.

  I will include a weekly review slot in each stage.

- <u>Specialist resources</u>: I could use an intervalometer to achieve a set of regular still images. I will use drawing from scientific manuals to explore the structure, as well as drawing from life.

> For your actual assessment, ask your tutor or check the latest Specification and Sample Assessment Material on the Pearson website for how long you have for different parts of the task, in order to prepare an appropriate time plan. Details of assessment may change, so always make sure you are up to date.

2 Using your preferred idea from those you identified on page 136, explain how you could work through this, from research to production. This could be in relation to the theme 'Structure' or to another theme you have worked with.

Use headings and the example on page 137 to help you respond to the areas you should address: initial ideas, reasons for choosing the art and design piece and the clear purpose, research plan (including reference to an artist or movement) and initial investigation, initial ideas on materials, techniques and processes, time plan, and any specialist equipment/resources you will need.

- <u>Idea</u>:

....

....

....

....

....

....

....

....

....

....

....

....

....

....

....

....

....

....

....

....

....

....

....

....

....

....

Links To revise generating, developing and recording ideas, see pages 134–138 of the Revision Guide.

Experimenting with ideas

Experimenting with ideas and **testing** them out is part of a structured process that should include consideration of your audience. This experimentation can help you develop and improve ideas for your final piece. Consider the factors below when structuring experimentation.

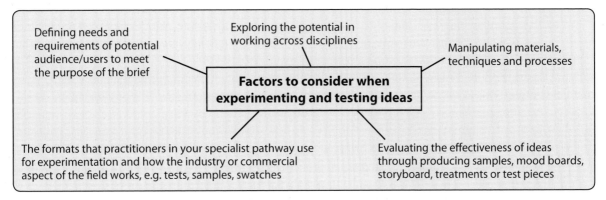

Defining needs and requirements of potential audience/users to meet the purpose of the brief

Exploring the potential in working across disciplines

Manipulating materials, techniques and processes

Factors to consider when experimenting and testing ideas

The formats that practitioners in your specialist pathway use for experimentation and how the industry or commercial aspect of the field works, e.g. tests, samples, swatches

Evaluating the effectiveness of ideas through producing samples, mood boards, storyboard, treatments or test pieces

Guided

1 Describe how you might use the above factors for your own experimentation and testing of ideas. Use headings to structure your response. You could relate this to 'Structure' or another theme you have worked with.

> In your actual assessment, experimentation and testing of ideas would contribute to your log and to your proposal, digital portfolio and written commentary, and support your final piece of work.

Experimenting and testing ideas

1 Define needs and requirements of potential audience/users to meet the purpose of the brief

With my idea ....

....

2 Explore the potential in working across disciplines/combining disciplines

....

....

3 Manipulate materials, techniques and processes

....

....

4 Evaluate the effectiveness of ideas through producing samples, mood boards, storyboard, treatments or test pieces

....

....

5 The formats that practitioners in my specialist pathway use for experimentation and any specialist expertise needed

....

....

Links To revise experimenting and testing ideas, see pages 135 and 139 of the Revision Guide.

Experimenting with Ms, Ts and Ps

Experimenting with different **materials**, **techniques** and **processes** is an important part of your creative response when generating ideas and selecting and applying them to produce a piece of art and design.

> Consider the following points in your experimentation.
> - Use drawings, diagrams, photographs or screengrabs to support your plan. Think about sourcing materials and how you will test your work, reflect on it and refine it. Planning your experimentation can yield exciting and unexpected results.
> - In any plan for creative output, you will need to include some time for review. Establish the sorts of questions to ask, to find out how it worked. Make sure you record your critical thinking on the experimentation.
> - Explore the format your experimentation could take. This will be related to your specialist pathway, any trends that inspire you in this pathway, and your choice of context for the revision task.
>
> In your actual assessment, you will need to keep an annotated log of the research and development of your ideas. This will ensure you have visual and written materials to select for your proposal, digital portfolio and written commentary, and to support your final piece of art and design.

1 Read the extract from a plan for experimentation below related to the theme of 'Structure', to help inform your own plan that follows on page 141.

- My plan is to explore the potential of photography, film, drawing and layering. I'm interested in layering techniques in both still and moving image – and I think I could add drama by exploring mark-making techniques to create a dark and foreboding sense of light. The exploratory work will need to:

    (a) be accurate in drawing and filming organic structures, with effective lighting and use of macro lenses, and

    (b) take risks in trying to communicate the idea of potential harm to structures, and so nature, from our industrial activities.

- There are different ways I could explore doing this. I could use exaggerated and heightened colour to emphasise an aspect of the structures I record. The drama in the message can be conveyed by experimenting with different techniques. For example, to show how chemicals can affect organic structures I could layer at least two sets of still/moving images – one of the structure, lit carefully, and one of dark ink in a tank of water slowly spreading out and over the structure. By combining these I could create the effect of a dark shadow or zone spreading across/throughout the structure and damaging it.

- Essentially, I need to experiment with getting good, well-composed and effectively recorded images, and at the same time explore alternative approaches, such as stop motion where the structure could be set up, filmed, stopped, slightly sprayed with a dark colour, filmed again, stopped and sprayed again, and so on.

2 Explain in more detail how you would take forward experimentation with materials, techniques and processes. Use your responses from pages 138 and 139 for practical experimentation based on the preferred idea you have identified. Use the above example and the work you have completed to help you.

> Describe the techniques and processes you might experiment with, justifying your choices. Depending on your specialism and theme, you could consider three of the following, for example: performance, process, interactive, sound, appropriation, movement.

- ....

....

....

....

....

....

....

....

....

....

....

....

....

....

....

....

....

....

....

....

....

....

....

Links To revise experimenting and testing ideas, see pages 135 and 139 of the Revision Guide.

Influences of practitioners on ideas

As part of your research and development of ideas, it is important to deconstruct and communicate the influence of the work of artists and designers on your own work and practice, and on trends. Consider their approach to a theme, and the way they use subject matter.

Use the activities below to consider the work of artists and designers from those listed in the brief on page 129 or the work of a recognised practitioner you are familiar with. The works could relate to the theme of 'Structure' or another theme you have worked with.

Guided

1 Choose one or two key pieces of work. Use the spidergram below to deconstruct the ways the chosen practitioners and works might inspire or influence your planning in relation to a theme, or influence a relevant trend. Tick the ways that have most inspired or influenced you.

In your actual assessment you can include the influences of practitioners in the explanation of your ideas in relation to the theme, your selection of research sources, and your explanation of the materials, techniques and processes you intend to use. You can record the influence in your annotated log, proposal, digital portfolio and written commentary, and use it to support your final piece of art and design.

It is useful to:
* use headings to clarify your thoughts
* be specific in explaining why they are an influence.

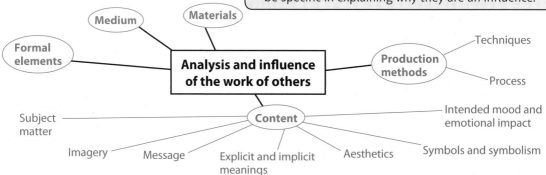

Guided

2 Explain why the chosen practitioners and their works are an influence on your ideas and work, or on a trend. Consider the approach to the theme and the subject matter. Refer to aspects you ticked in the spidergram above.

Approach to the theme: I have gained inspiration and ideas based on the way others have interpreted and communicated the theme. I can see how their interpretation is both similar and different from my own.

Here is an extract of an explanation about subject matter relating to the theme of 'Structure':

I'm interested in the way structure is used in their work. They use a subject that is all around us and often literally underpins what and who we are. They have represented structure in different ways and use it to suggest thought-provoking nuances. I think this may be due to our understanding of how important structure is, and how essentially incredible some organic structures are, such as the fractal principle.

For example, ...

....

....

Approach to subject matter: ....

....

....

Links To revise practitioner influences, see pages 136 and 149–159 of the Revision Guide.

Contextual influences on ideas

You can support ideas generation and practical experimentation with information and understanding gained from **historical**, **contemporary**, **social**, **economic**, **political** and **cultural** research.

> **Contextual influences** can be defined as the impact of other factors on a creative practitioner's work, such as the time or era that work was produced, or any political, social and cultural influences.

> Identify how you would plan contextual research for your preferred idea based on the theme 'Structure' or a theme you have worked with. In your actual assessment, you can include contextual influences in the explanation of your ideas in relation to the theme, your selection of research sources, and your explanation of the materials, techniques and processes you intend to use. You can record the influence in your annotated log, proposal, digital portfolio and written commentary, and use it to support your final piece of art and design.

1   Read the examples of plans for contextual research in relation to the theme of 'Structure'. Pay attention to the influence from art and design sources and non-art sources. This will help you identify your own approaches in your plans that follow.

Contextual research into two art and design sources

1   For primary research I am going to visit an exhibition that features examples of new approaches to work, including an artist I want to investigate, Shane Hope. He uses 3D printed and worked up surfaces in paintings and constructions, referencing organic structures.

2   I am also going to a museum where there is a section on small-scale drawings of botanical forms, some recent and some Victorian, which I think might be examples of closely observed natural structures. I will record using drawing, colour and photography. I am also researching artists and designers that have explored structure, including painters, as well as designers that have used organic forms in their work, from furniture by Ron Arad to printed textiles.

Contextual research into two non-art and design sources

1   I am contacting a local horticultural college to see if they have any examples of organic structures I can photograph, i.e. in a hot house – they may even have the potential to scan structures in the college.

2   I am also looking at scientific manuals based on organic biology, and emailing science teachers in this field to ask if they have any relevant materials.

2 Outline **two art and design sources** and **two non-art and design sources** that you could research in relation to your specialism and the theme of 'Structure' or another theme you have worked with.

<u>Contextual research into two art and design sources</u>

1 ....

....

....

....

....

....

....

2 ....

....

....

....

....

....

<u>Contextual research into two non-art and design sources</u>

1 ....

....

....

....

....

....

....

2 ....

....

....

....

....

....

....

 Links To revise contextual influences, see pages 136 and 143–159 of the Revision Guide.

Planning your proposal

Your research and development of initial ideas will inform your plans for your **proposal** to create a piece of art and design in a **discipline of your choice**, with a **clear purpose**.

> Ask your tutor or check the Pearson website for the most up-to-date Sample Assessment Material to find out which activities are supervised or unsupervised in your actual assessment, how long you have and whether you can take any research and preparatory work into the supervised assessment. The details of the actual assessed task may change so always make sure you are up to date.

Use the questions below to outline the **key points** of a proposal showing how you intend to respond to the theme 'Structure' or another theme you have worked with.

1   Describe your initial ideas for the focus of your art and design piece (see pages 131–139).

> Explain your ideas in relation to the theme, your design discipline of choice and the clear purpose (for example, a piece of artwork for an exhibition, advertising or promotional material, interactive product, commercial design/product, functional object, fashion garment or accessory).

....

....

....

....

....

....

....

2   Explain the reasons for your choice of art and design piece (see pages 136–139).

> Explain the reasons behind your choice of art and design piece. Define your intention and what you are going to communicate.

....

....

....

....

....

....

3   Outline your research plan into contextual sources and trends (see pages 142–144).

> Include and explain your selection of relevant sources and the research you have carried out so far, as evidenced in your log. Refer to contextual sources and trends from your primary, secondary and contextual sources, how they combine, and their influence.

....

....

....

....

....

....

....

4 Explain your initial ideas on the materials, techniques and processes you want to use (see pages 140–141).

> Explain why you have chosen the materials, techniques and processes and include your ideas arising from experimentation.

....

....

....

....

....

....

....

....

5 Explain how you plan to complete the work within the allocated time (see page 147).

> Break your work down into stages with interim deadlines that can be completed within the time constraints. Make sure it is specific, measurable, achievable, realistic, time-bound (SMART). You could use a week-by-week plan.

....

....

....

....

....

....

....

....

....

6 Identify any equipment and specialist expertise you may require (see page 139).

> Consider anything you need for your specialism. For example, you might have needs related to sewing, print room, screens, mannequins, and so on.

....

....

....

....

....

....

....

Links To revise producing a proposal, see pages 140–142 of the Revision Guide.

Identifying scope and timescales

To make sure you can achieve what you set out in your proposal, you need to plan your time carefully.

Guided

1 Consider a **time plan** that breaks the brief into **specific stages**. Make **key notes** on what sort of activities you would schedule, with what resources and aims. Refer to the brief on pages 125–130 and be specific. Use additional pages if needed. This could relate to the theme of 'Structure' or another theme you have worked with.

> Ask your tutor or check the Pearson website for the most up-to-date Sample Assessment Material to find out how much time you have for different parts in your actual assessment. The details of the actual assessed task may change so always make sure you are up to date.

What I will be doing	Resources required	Notes	Session/week
Research – into theme	Library/internet/visit	Needs definition: obvious/literal & alternative	
Contextual research – using examples	Out for recording primary sources	Widest possible range of sources/ fields; keep options open; record for context & creative	

 Links To revise managing your time, see pages 141–142 and 170 of the Revision Guide.

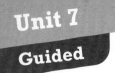

Developing contextual research

You will **continue to develop the contextual research** from your planning and proposal with your **practical work** for your piece of art and design.

> **Guided**

1 Describe different ways that contextual research from art and non-art sources can be developed into practical work using the specific techniques and media that you planned in earlier. Start with drawing and photography.

> Use headings to show the different methods, and then explain these. For example, you might use drawing to develop your contextual research by recording, and give specific examples. You might then use photography to explore in different ways. This could relate to the theme of 'Structure' or another theme you have worked with. In your actual assessment you could select from records such as these to include them in your digital portfolio and written commentary, and to support your final piece of art and design.

Drawing

Drawing can be used as a way of recording from primary contextual sources and then developed into drawing-based ideas. The actual drawing made on the spot can be used for this. Drawing can also be used to analyse others' use of formal elements, and then used to inform the development process. This can give a strong understanding of just how practitioners use formal elements and visual language in their work. My use of drawing to develop my contextual research in response

to the theme ....

....

....

....

....

Photography

....

....

....

....

2 Choose a further method that is relevant for your specialism. Explain why you have chosen it and how you could use it to develop your contextual research and piece of art and design.

> Consider the different types of research:
> * Visual research – selecting, observing and recording of visual resources
> * Action research – practical experimentation with techniques and processes
> * Academic research – gathering information about practitioners and their working practice

....

....

....

....

....

 Links To revise developing contextual research, see pages 136 and 143–159 of the Revision Guide.

Recording work in progress

As you continue to develop, review and refine your ideas and practical work based on your planning, proposal and the production process, continue to **record your work in progress**.

When recording work in progress, consider the following points:
- Make sure you record the **key developments** of your work. Consider the benefits of different ways of recording and try out which ones work best for your purposes, including annotating your visuals. Show your critical thinking, refinements and decision-making.
- **Summarise** your information and use the **correct terminology**.
- Your use of photography and drawing at this stage is different from when generating ideas and recording source materials. Make the images **clear** and arrange them with **purpose**.
- If you are working digitally, **back up** your images and information.

In your actual assessment you could select from records such as these for inclusion in your digital portfolio and written commentary, and use them to support your final piece of art and design.

Guided

1 Review the sketchbook page below, which uses written description and photography to record a process and demonstrate a work in progress. List **two** benefits of using these methods to record a process.

(a) Written description can be used to describe the key stages in a process, and clarify the sequence of events or activities.

(b) ....

PAPER MAKING

- I bought a Financial Times newspaper as it was pink instead of normal black and white – this gave paper more of a brown colour, which I prefer.
- The first step was to rip the paper into many small pieces;
- The torn pieces were combined with water in a deep tray and left to soak overnight;
- Once soaked, the paper was scooped out in small amounts and placed into the blender – with twice as much water to paper added to the mix;
- The paper was thoroughly blended until it was a smooth pulp, and then poured into another tray;
- Additional trays were used to make different types of paper pulp, again with water added to the halfway mark on the side of the tray – without this water the pulp would have been too thick;
- The pulp was further stirred to stop the fibres settling too early before being added to the deckle;
- The deckle was held at 45 degrees and the pulp mixture was pushed into it – the deckle needed to be submerged partly in water at times to make sure the pulp could be spread around;
- The deckle was then lifted out of the tray and the water allowed to drain out;
- It was placed on a cloth and other items were added and pressed into it;
- Another cloth was placed on top, and pressure applied evenly, and a sponge used to take out excess water;
- After a short while, the deckle could be turned over and tapped gently to release the paper, which was allowed to air-dry naturally.

Materials and equipment -
Waste paper
Mold or Deckle
Liquidiser/bowl
Plastic tray – deep
Re-usable kitchen cloth
Objects to impress into pulp

Record of paper making.

2 Review the set of images below. They show the recording of a painting idea using painterly techniques based on a landscape idea and reflection, through recording different versions of the idea. Describe how you think the idea is developing from image 1 to image 4.

1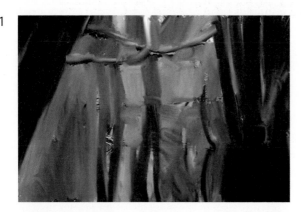

2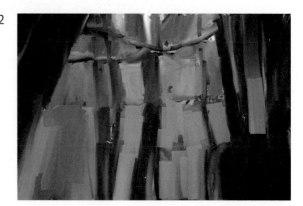

3

4

Set of images recording different versions of an idea. Winter Land 1, 2, 3, 4 – four studies, physical and digital painting.

....

....

....

....

....

....

....

....

....

....

....

....

....

....

 Links To revise selecting, recording, reviewing and refining ideas, see pages 160–169 of the Revision Guide.

Exploring development through the production process

You will continue to develop your practical work based on your planning and proposal as you review and refine through the creative process. This includes exploring the development of work through the production process.

> Developing work through the production process will involve the plans you have made earlier in relation to materials, techniques and processes, for example. Think about how you will test these out practically to develop your work.
>
> Consider the following:
> - Design sheets or screengrabs
> - Short film, games or animation clips, photographs
> - Models and maquettes
> - Toiles
> - Samples/drafts/working drawings
>
> In your actual assessment you could select records such as these to include in your digital portfolio and written commentary, and to support your final piece of art and design.

1   Select **two** of the ways above and evaluate their potential effectiveness in recording the development of your practical work in your response to the theme 'Structure' or another theme you have worked with.

1   ....
....
....
....
....
....
....
....
....

2   ....
....
....
....
....
....
....
....

 Links   To revise developing and managing the production process, see page 166 of the Revision Guide.

Reviewing and refining ideas

You will continue to review and refine your ideas and practical work based on your planning, proposal and the production process.

> In your actual assessment you could select from records such as these for inclusion in your digital portfolio and written commentary, and use them to support your final piece of art and design.

1 Identify **one** key page of preparatory work you have produced in the development stage relating to the theme of 'Structure' or another theme you have worked with. Describe and evaluate the processes and techniques you used in the work shown on the page.

....

....

....

....

....

....

....

....

....

2 Explain how you can develop your practical work based on the information and potential of the work on your selected page of preparatory work.

> You can review and refine ideas through:
> • reviewing the potential and evolution of ideas
> • reflecting on the strengths and weaknesses of ideas
> • planning to adapt or change things to improve.

....

....

....

....

....

....

....

....

....

🔗 **Links** To revise reviewing and refining ideas, see pages 167–169 of the Revision Guide.

Reflecting on progress

A key part of continuing to develop, review and refine your ideas and practical work is to **reflect on progress.** Apply critical reflection to analyse and evaluate the progress of your work. In your actual assessment you could select from records such as these for inclusion in your digital portfolio and written commentary, and use them to support your final piece of art and design.

> Reflect on the two images below, which are part of a series of giclée prints exploring a combination of photography, physical and digital drawing. In these images the basis for experimentation was mark making and colour.
> - The context was of images exploring a theme of 'Pathway', where the idea of a river cutting a path through the landscape/townscape was developed.
> - These images are part of a series where mark making was being developed to explore and experiment with making the combined photographs and drawings more distinct and visually arresting.

 Guided

1 Complete the annotation of the visual analysis of these two images, based on the information you have been given.

Describe the way marks have been used in this image.

The mark making uses darker colours on

top of ....

....

Describe the effect of the mark making.

The overall effect of the mark making seems to emphasise the horizontal movement or ripples in the water, in a slightly expressive though still

naturalistic way ....

....

Compare the two images – describe how the colour in this image is different, and where it remained the same.

....

....

....

Explain the effect of the colour range on this image, for example to communicate a 'mood' or a different feeling to the other image.

....

....

....

Bedford River 12 and Bedford River 14, 2015, photography, digital drawing and painting, and printmaking.

 Links To revise reflection and review, see pages 167–169 of the Revision Guide.

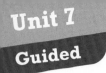

Planning to adapt or change

In response to your reflection on the progress and development of your work, you will need plans to adapt or change things in your practical work, to **improve** it. Take a structured approach, and be specific. In your actual assessment you could select from records such as these for inclusion in your digital portfolio and written commentary, and use them to support your final piece of art and design.

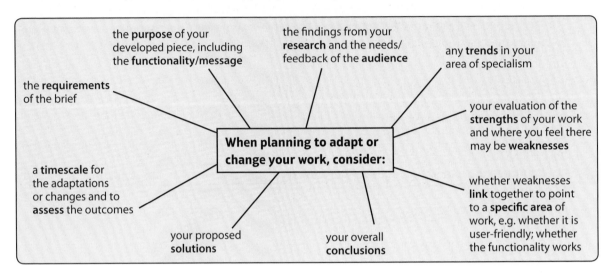

1 Select a piece of work you have reviewed in relation to the theme of 'Structure' or another theme you have worked with.

Use the points in the spidergram above to explain either:
- how you would plan to adapt or change a current piece of work, to improve it
- how you have already adapted and changed a piece of work and improved it.

....

....

....

....

....

....

....

....

....

....

....

....

....

Links To revise reviewing and creating solutions, see pages 167–169 of the Revision Guide.

Completing final piece to deadline

You will need a **time plan** when producing your final piece of work. Take account of all the relevant considerations, including the needs of your specialism. You can build on the planning in relation to timescales and considerations that you identified in your proposal (pages 145–147).

> Take into account the number and complexity of the tasks overall, such as ordering resources, exposure times or drying times. You may need to book time to use specific equipment or facilities. Plan the sequence and timing of your activities so that you make best use of time to achieve the deadline.

Guided > **1** Use the headings below to show how you would address these considerations for completing a final piece of work to deadline. You could use your work in relation to the theme of 'Structure' or another theme you have worked with.

<u>Taking account of the use of chosen materials, techniques and processes</u>

....

....

....

....

<u>Considering timescales to prepare elements of work related to specialism, e.g. drying, firing, rendering</u>

....

....

....

....

<u>Meeting health and safety requirements</u>

....

....

> Consider risk assessment and working safely in different environments, and requirements in relation to the final piece produced.

....

....

....

<u>Sourcing specialist technical equipment and assistance</u>

....

....

....

....

> **Links** To revise considerations in completing work to deadline, see pages 170–172 of the Revision Guide.

Realising your final piece of work

Realising your final piece of work brings together your research, development and practical work in **producing a piece of art and design** with a clear purpose, in a specialism of your choice, that meets the brief.

Your realised final piece needs to show:
- accuracy of construction or fluent application of media
- fullest interpretation of development work
- modifications that have been considered
- quality issues that have been addressed
- fitness for purpose
- reflection of the planned intention.

1 Create a checklist, which could be used as you realise a piece of work, to assess how far you are demonstrating each of the above points your realised piece needs to show.

....

....

....

These will determine the quality of your final piece. You could break each point down into key relevant points. For example, you could consider how the piece is meeting the needs of the audience and addressing any constraints. You could refer to your research to think about how this could be measured.

You could use your work in relation to any theme you work with. In your actual assessment you could select from records such as these for inclusion in your digital portfolio and written commentary.

....

....

....

....

....

....

....

....

....

....

....

....

....

....

....

....

 Links To revise realising the final piece, see pages 173–177 of the Revision Guide.

Producing a portfolio

To produce a **portfolio that demonstrates your development and realisation process**, you will need to photograph or scan selected pieces of development work and of the final piece to include in your digital portfolio. Selecting relevant images and commentary is vital to the way your project will be seen and reviewed. You may also wish to consider the content of your **written commentary** alongside this work (see pages 161–162).

> The revision brief on pages 126–127 includes the following requirements for the digital portfolio:
> - Must be between 16 and 20 pages.
> - Each page can include a combination of images and written work.
> - Select key pieces of your development work to include.
> - Select images of your art and design piece.
> - Produce written annotations explaining your development process.
> - Produce images of your final art and design piece.
>
> Ask your tutor or check the Pearson website for the most up-to-date Sample Assessment Material to find out any requirements for a portfolio in your actual assessment. The details of the actual assessed task may change so always make sure you are up to date.

> Consider key pieces of **development work** and images of the **final art and design piece** to include. This could be on the theme of 'Structure' or another theme you have worked with.

Guided

1 List **three** factors that may determine how you select imagery and annotation that shows your **creative response to the theme** (see pages 131–148).

(a) To show a wide range of ideas generation.

(b) ....

(c) ....

Guided

2 List **three** factors that may determine how you select imagery and annotation that shows your use of **contextual sources and influences** in your work (see pages 137–146).

(a) To show the specific contextual examples and sources I used and how they relate to the theme.

(b) ....

(c) ....

Guided

3 List **three** factors that may determine how you select imagery and annotation that shows your **exploration of materials, techniques and processes** in your development work (see pages 137–142).

(a) To show examples of tests, samples, maquettes, models, mock-ups, roughs.

(b) ....

(c) ....

Guided 4 List **three** factors that may determine your selection of imagery and annotation that shows how you **refine your work through review and evaluation** (see pages 149–154).

> Think about what exactly you want the page to show.

(a) To show critical reflection through comment and annotation.

(b) ....

(c) ....

Guided 5 List **three** factors that may determine your selection of imagery and annotation that allows your portfolio to show well all the **development and realisation processes** (see pages 155–158).

(a) To make sure all the stages in the development processes are presented.

(b) ....

(c) ....

Guided 6 List **three** factors that may determine the quality of **presentation of the portfolio**.

(a) To take care when mounting my work.

(b) ....

(c) ....

7 Consider points 1–6 above. Choose one of these and describe how you would set up a portfolio page that shows the imagery and annotation for the factors you have listed.

....

....

....

....

....

....

....

....

....

....

....

....

....

....

....

Links To revise producing a portfolio, see pages 178–179 of the Revision Guide.

Recording images for a portfolio

When the process of selecting images and accompanying annotation is complete, you will need to **edit** different images and bring them together on the pages of the portfolio in a way that shows the points you are making. You may also wish to consider the content of your **written commentary** alongside this work (see pages 161–162).

When considering how images for a portfolio page show a related focus, you will need to do the following:

1 Select a stage in your project. Use the practical work you have completed and the considerations from pages 157–158. You **must** have different images that you can combine.

2 Select and list images to be combined and explain why you have selected these.

3 Practise combining images together in software on a single portfolio page, making notes on what you feel are important factors to consider.

4 Think about position, layout, scale and legibility of any text when producing a portfolio page.

Ask your tutor or check the Pearson website for the most up-to-date Sample Assessment Material to find out any requirements for a portfolio in your actual assessment. The details of the actual assessed task may change so always make sure you are up to date.

1   Select **three images on a single focus**. You could use your work from pages 157–158 and practical work you have completed in relation to 'Structure' or another theme you have worked with. For each image:

• explain why you have selected it

• make key notes for the accompanying annotation.

Image 1 ....

....

....

....

....

....

Image 2 ....

....

....

....

....

....

Image 3 ....

....

....

....

....

....

2 Practise combining the images in software. Add to the mind maps below any factors you feel are important to be considered when working on this task to create a professional portfolio.

> Ask your tutor or check the Pearson website for the most up-to-date Sample Assessment Material to find out any requirements in relation to hardware and software for a portfolio in your actual assessment. The details of the actual assessed task may change so always make sure you are up to date.

Work to be accessed digitally to be in correct format, e.g. PDF documents

Size to show quality of the work

3D and larger pieces to be photographed, including indication of scale

Considerations for recording examples of visual work for a portfolio

Set up a photo shoot in a dedicated space

Backgrounds, lighting, positioning, alternative views

Professional practice when compiling portfolios (e.g. research portfolios/ web of practitioners; portfolio requirements for Higher Education; choose and present images to meet requirements of brief)

Use preview facilities, evaluate success or weakness during shoot progress

Scan and import flat images using flatbed scanner

Size of moving image files, output format

Organise data transfer via SD card, hard drive, USB pen

Use software to capture images and output as contact sheets

Make final decision on work, refine or further shoot if required

Capturing and editing digital work

Control file size and resolution depending on destination

Digital format, use correct file naming protocols, import and/or export images

Use image manipulation tools in software to edit images

3 How would you ensure all the images are well lit and clear?

> This is a blend of technique and use of equipment.

....

....

....

....

4 Find an example of a portfolio that most closely reflects what you want yours to do. Explain the layout and communication methods it employs, and what you learn from it.

....

....

....

....

....

Links To revise images in your portfolio, see pages 179–187 of the Revision Guide.

Planning a written commentary

Your selection of images and annotation for the portfolio will inform your plans for a written commentary of the design and realisation process to accompany each page of the portfolio.

> Ask your tutor or check the Pearson website for the most up-to-date Sample Assessment Material to find out which activities are supervised or unsupervised in your actual assessment, how long you have and whether you can take any research and preparatory work into the supervised assessment. Pay attention to whether the commentary must be handwritten in a booklet provided. The details of the actual assessed task may change so always make sure you are up to date.

> The written commentary of your design and realisation process to accompany each page of your digital portfolio should include:
> * explanations of your development process
> * explanations of how you achieved your final piece and how it responds to the theme
> * an evaluation of the development process and the final piece of work.

Guided

1 Make a list of how you might divide the work completed for the task across the total number of pages, by subject or stage. You can use the theme of 'Structure' or another theme you have worked with. Consider the following points:
* the revision task, which requests one commentary per portfolio page and between 16 and 20 pages in total
* the points in the hint box above, which outline what should be included in your written commentary
* the points considered for pages of the portfolio (pages 157–160) and how they might match the points above
* the overall structure of the written commentary in relation to the imagery and annotation you have selected – consider the impact of your opening and closing pages, and how to show your journey in meeting the brief

Page 1: definition of theme, clear purpose and chosen specialism ....

....

Page 2: ....

....

Page 3: ....

....

Page 4: ....

....

Page 5: ....

....

Page 6: ....

....

Page 7: ....

....

Page 8: ....

....

Page 9: ....

....

Page 10: ....

....

Page 11: ....

....

Page 12: ....

....

Page 13: ....

....

Page 14: ....

....

Page 15: ....

....

Page 16: ....

....

2 Write down **four** ways you can show your creative response to a theme for inclusion in a commentary on a portfolio page. Consider your clear purpose, your specialism and ways you consider the audience needs.

(a) ....

(b) ....

(c) ....

(d) ....

3 Using the work you have completed, write a commentary for a chosen single page of your portfolio. It can relate to the theme of 'Structure' or another theme you have worked with.

....

....

....

....

....

....

....

....

....

> Aim to spend no more than ten minutes writing a commentary for any one portfolio page. Consider how you will demonstrate the quality of your written commentary, including:
> * clear explanations that demonstrate the strengths and qualities of the work, engage the audience and show clear development of work and ideas
> * accurate use of spelling, grammar and specialist terminology.

....

....

....

....

....

....

....

....

Links To revise planning a portfolio and written commentary, see pages 178–188 of the Revision Guide.

Revision activities

Ask your tutor or check the up-to-date Sample Assessment Material on the Pearson website to get an indication of the structure of your actual assessed task and what this requires of you. Pay attention to whether Activity 2 and Activity 5 are supervised activities, and the time allowed for them. The details of the actual assessed task may change so always make sure you are up to date.

Although the revision task refers to researching, developing and realising creative intentions in response to a brief for a piece of art and design that has a clear purpose with a theme of 'Structure', the activities in this Workbook will only require you to focus on the skills associated with the tasks. You are **not** expected to undertake full research, development and production of a piece of art and design nor associated tasks such as a full proposal, portfolio and commentary. Although the theme in the revision brief is 'Structure', the activities in this Workbook may also involve a wider range of examples to demonstrate skills that you can apply with any theme.

Revision activity 2

Consider how you would produce a proposal explaining how you intend to respond to the theme to produce a piece of art and design in a discipline of your choice and with a clear purpose.

The proposal must include details on:

- your initial ideas for the focus of your art and design piece
- the reasons for your choice of art and design piece
- your research plan into contextual sources and trends
- your initial ideas on the materials, techniques and processes you want to use
- your plans to complete the work within the time
- identification of the equipment and specialist expertise you may require.

Make sure you demonstrate your skills in:

- explanation of ideas in relation to the theme
- selection of research sources
- explanation of the materials, techniques and processes you intend to use.

> ✏ Write a brief proposal, using the headings and areas you have planned around in this Workbook (see pages 145–146) to structure your response in relation to 'Structure' or another theme you have worked with.

....
....
....
....
....
....
....
....
....
....
....

Revision activity 5

Consider how you would produce a commentary of your development and realisation process to accompany each page of your digital portfolio.

This should include:

- explanations of your development processes (including identification of key stages and how you used these to inform the progress of your project, for example review of initial research)
- explanations of how you achieved your final piece and how it responds to the theme
- an evaluation of the development process and the final piece of work.

Make sure you demonstrate your skills in:

- the quality and clarity of your explanation
- accurate use of spelling, grammar and subject-specific terminology.

> ✎ Using the structure and areas you have planned around in this Workbook for the portfolio and the written commentary (pages 157–162) write a commentary on a portfolio page of your choice in relation to 'Structure' or another theme you have worked with. Aim to spend no more than ten minutes writing a commentary for any one portfolio page.

....

....

....

....

....

....

....

....

....

....

....

....

....

....

....

....

....

....

....

....

Answers

Unit 1: Visual Recording and Communication

Interpreting a brief (page 6)

1 Individual responses reflecting your own specialism and interests.

Additional ideas might include, for example:
- judicial system (jail bars, handcuffs, police)
- medicine (tablets, syringe, face mask, plaster)
- homes (bamboo hut, treehouse, camper van, tent)
- automotive (airbags, seatbelts, crash helmets, windscreen).

There are no right or wrong answers, but you will want others to recognise how the things you include are connected to the theme. If single words don't make sense to others, you might want to include some further details of how you think it connects.

2 Individual responses reflecting your own specialism and interests.

Researching a theme (pages 7–8)

1 Individual responses.

Bear in mind the following guidance:
- Research widely so that you can inform your work from a broad spectrum of art and design disciplines: your selected artists should be from quite different disciplines such as product design and fashion.
- While work often connects to multiple themes and doesn't have to explicitly visualise protection, the audience should widely recognise the connection of the work to the theme.
- The explanation you give for selecting the artwork should move beyond issues related to whether you like it and focus on what you can learn from it. For example, in the sample extract below:

Andy Warhol, Electric Chair, 1964: I picked the Electric Chair by Warhol because of my interest in ideas of protection in relation to human rights. Warhol has presented a direct visual of an object related to taking someone's life, which is a highly controversial act that still takes place in democratic societies. Yet, it is used to protect society from criminals to a certain extent so the connection to the theme is twofold.

2 Individual responses.

3 Individual responses, considering the following:
- It is important that the making process is evident within the final artwork that you choose.
- The audience needs to recognise how a part of the artwork connects to something that has been observed in existence through its recording. It might be quite obvious – drawings are literal visual recordings, but artists also use very inventive ways of recording such as taking rubbings, samples or even recording a process and action rather than an object.
- Your explanation needs to easily describe:
  ○ what was recorded
  ○ how it has been recorded
  ○ how the above communicates the theme.

4 Individual responses. Your answers should show a good spread of different examples from history, demonstrating an awareness of how visual recording has evolved and changed. Your explanation should reference how the technique for recording has evolved. For example, in the extracts below:
- Vermeer innovated in the field of visual recording by employing a camera obscura literally to copy the projection of the real world and develop a level of accuracy in his paintings. While artists had used measuring techniques previously, this was early use of lens technology and understanding of light.

- Richard Long would document the act of walking through the desert by making marks with his feet directly into the ground. This left long lines that he was able to capture with a camera later. This was a radical departure from methods of recording used traditionally within the arts and helped broaden the understanding of recording an experience or movement.

Visual recording and communication of content (pages 9–11)

Individual responses that might include the following points.

1 Individual choice of image.

2 Theme:
Make sure you reference the specific formal elements within the composition as a whole. Link them with how protection is formally communicated. Some example extracts follow.

Image 1:
- Each of the items is illustrated in clear bold lines. The simple illustration means they are removed from context, and focus the viewers' attention on exactly their function. They all relate to containing or to holding together, which are means of protecting the contents from making a mess or spoiling.
- The artist has illustrated the work using only outlines and this makes the objects transparent. The layering effect suggests that the items are puncturing each other and are not solid in the way they are expected to be. This makes them appear fragile and without an outer skin for protection.

Image 2:
- The shape and scale of the water dominate the composition and provide a threatening sense of danger and vulnerability to the viewer. This makes the viewer feel unprotected within the elements.
- Lighthouses are synonymous with the idea of protecting people at sea. However, the artist has painted the lighthouse very small within the landscape to show how nature is far more powerful than anything people can create.

3 Ideas:
At this stage, your analysis should rely on specific references to the medium used within the artwork. You will need to explain how the medium used, and how it is applied, communicates the idea within the image. Some example extracts follow.

Image 1:
- Each of the objects are painted in a graphic solid line method that is enabled through working on a surface like aluminium. Such sharp lines and shiny surface are reminiscent of protective signage used in the transport industry, such as aeroplane safety guides. As most people have seen these safety guides, they will associate this type of illustrative work with protection.

Image 2:
- The reduced colour palette created by the wash and crayons replicates what would widely be accepted as stormy weather, hurricanes and an inhospitable environment. The movement in the shapes of the waves created by brushstrokes contributes to the sense of wind and danger.

4 Context:
Before embarking on ideas generation of their own, artists and designers often research the history and context of a theme. This is because themes and ideas, such as protection, change throughout history. For example, human rights as a statute did not always exist and laws have changed that protect people to a far more significant extent. Artists and designers research how this has changed to inform their work with ideas that might challenge current notions of protection.

Your answers should include references to well-known historic events that relate to issues connected to politics, religion, environment or technology. Some examples might include the following:
- In the Stone Age, people lived in caves for protection before technologies advanced to enable home building.

- The Cold War forced the development of increasingly destructive weapons as a form of deterrent, and mutual destruction as a method of protection.
- The advances in computer technology and our continued reliance on technology within our day-to-day lives focus our attention on cyber threats and artificial intelligence as opposed to tangible and physical forces.
- Changes in weather patterns due to global warming make the weather less predictable and more concerning in day-to-day life.

Understanding and exploring form (page 12)

1 Individual responses.
   When analysing the formal elements, your answers will need to:
   - reference the specific formal elements including line, tone, form, texture, colour, pattern, scale, perspective, figure and ground or composition in the work. Ideally, you will discuss multiple formal elements and explain how these work together to communicate.
   - explain how the formal elements in the work connect to the theme. The answer could discuss how a change in the formal elements would change how the work communicates to help clarify the argument.

2 When analysing form, you will also explore the purpose and use of a piece.
   - Design work will have been created for a specific function and purpose.
   - This may be readily connected to a theme, for example 'Protection'.
   - When analysing form, purpose and use, make the connection to theme explicit and go into some detail about relationship to the theme.
   - Historic artwork may have had a specific purpose and function socially and you should be aware of what this was.
   - For more contemporary artwork, you can consider the types of debates it may relate to and what questions it provokes in the viewer, as these reflect its purpose.

Understanding and exploring process (page 13)

1 Individual responses. Each of the three images should present a clear connection to each of material, technique and process. Analysis might include the following, for example, in relation to the theme of 'Protection'.
   Material:
   Your image may have an overt relationship to the theme, such as being used in the act of protection itself such as metal or Kevlar. It could support the interpretation of protection through its formal element of colour, texture or pattern. The material may also show qualities for protection or its antithesis of fragility.
   Technique:
   The technique you have chosen may be clearly visible within the craftsmanship, or you may have to show knowledge of its construction process. If it isn't clear, then you may want to make it evident in the title or annotation. The technique employed should contribute to your ideas for your own artwork and you should be able to describe how the technique relates to the theme. The way you manipulate paint with a brush will leave specific marks that may feel strong and bold or fragile and delicate, for example.
   Process:
   The process employed within the work you have chosen will not always be evident from the image and you will often have to demonstrate background knowledge of the creative process of the work. Your discussion of the process will have to show multiple stages of production. It may be that the artefact itself has been through a process of techniques. It may also be that the work drew on a series of activities or iterations before it was realised. It may also be that the image doesn't demonstrate an outcome, because the work may have been a process or activity, rather than a final object. This may be the case for performance or site-specific work, for example.

2 Individual responses. Your analysis should, for example:
   - use the terminology of material, technique or process and show that you understand the differences between these
   - demonstrate some research into the work itself and have knowledge of the specific materials, techniques and processes used within the work
   - explain how the material, technique or process might inform your own work and ideas for your own project.

Understanding and exploring mood (page 14)

Individual responses, taking into account the considerations below, for example, which use the theme of 'Protection'.

1 When selecting a picture that communicates a protection mood, you will need to be confident that you and others will be able to understand the same interpretation of the image, in relation to the theme. The mood related to the theme of protection will generally be presented in an image of either strength, fragility, danger or care.

2 A valuable way of interpreting work is through the mood it communicates. Your insights into the work can start with very personal feelings about the way it affects you. However, you should be able to identify and use visual language terminology to justify your arguments. Answers that are based on more than one formal element and visual communication will be more reliable and ensure that the interpretation is shared by the audience.

3 Example response extract:
   I would describe my work and its intentions as a collage that tries to communicate issues related to our environment and how it is being endangered by using harsh cutting techniques and thin slices of image.
   I chose colour to impact on the audience by making sure that the colour was widely recognised as connecting to the theme of protection and related to artefacts people encounter in day-to-day life.
   When considering texture, it was important to find a smooth surface that replicated metal, which is something that feels solid and impenetrable.
   The material I chose to impact on the audience was nails, as these were unusual to see in an artwork and generated a feeling of pain and threat, making the audience feel vulnerable.

Application and meaning (page 15)

1 Individual responses that might consider the following points:
   - Explanations should reference an aspect of the materials, techniques or processes that have gone into creating the work. Ideally, you should research and read about the way the artist has made the work and not only rely on a purely visual reading from an image.
   - Explanations could include the way the image would communicate if it included only painted butterflies, in a purely decorative way. You could compare this to the use of real butterflies in the actual paintings.
   - Look up the image on the internet, consider the placement of the butterflies and reflect on debates about whether this could be classed as painting in the strictest sense as Hirst is clearly trying to break some of the boundaries of traditional painting methods.

2 Individual responses that should look at the composition of the image and focus on connections between elements in the image and what these communicate when combined. For example, by placing the handprint on a barrier, the artist has drawn our attention to:
   - physical barriers in our environment
   - the difference between our man-made manufactured environment and organic human bodies
   - issues and debates relating to segregation and immigration.

3 Individual responses that should focus on what the work communicates to a broad audience. Consider, for example:
   - materials: what these might communicate to an audience and how they have been applied or combined

- techniques: whether these are traditional or non-traditional methods and how this might impact on the communication
- processes: whether the meaning would be different if the audience was not aware of the process behind creating the work.

Understanding and exploring formal elements (page 16)
Individual choices of works of art or design that relate to the formal elements of line, colour and composition, using different visual recording techniques to record them.

The formal element indicated in the boxes should be easily recognised from the image. While all images will have colour, and most will have line, you will need to be confident that others will be able to judge the image as emphasising the formal elements you associate with it.

It is important that your own exploration of the formal elements within others' work is broad and sustained. This will come through trying different media and approaches, rather than sticking with just a few.

Visual recording from non-art (page 17)
1–2 Individual choices of at least two forms of abstract visual data with an explanation of their relationship to the theme. Ensuring you look at non-art and abstract data forms will mean that you are underpinning your interpretation of the theme with valuable knowledge. There is a great opportunity to look at historic and current data that often provides fresh insight and a visual interpretation of things that are not literally visible. You can use internet searches as a starting point, but should not just take the top results. Try to move towards wider primary and secondary sources. Your explanation should connect the formal elements in the image with an interpretation of the meaning and how these combine to inform your own work or understanding of the theme. Ideally, you will explain how the images and information inform your own creative ideas.

Informing your own practice (page 18)
1 Individual responses. Some types of visual recording are obvious within an image. Photorealist images are a clear example of visual recording. However, for others you may need to undertake some background research to see how visual recording supports their practice. Methods used by artists and designers include the following:
  (a) Sketching and drawing from observations are an obvious example. These might include drawing from scenes or objects, but they could also include staged poses and still lives that have been set up.
  (b) Taking rubbings or imprints from objects and surfaces can give artists a different insight and these can be used later on as part of artwork.
  (c) Artists and designers frequently use photography to visually explore and record objects and scenes. They may also use experimental methods of photography such as pinhole cameras or photograms to capture images.
  (d) Experimental methods of mark making used by artists and designers to record alternative views. These might include drawing using the wrong hand or continuous line drawing. While these don't offer exact replicas, they enable a creative and gestural observation.
  (e) Some artists and designers will use their body as a tool for recording, such as making prints or marks on surfaces or the environment.
2 Individual responses that may reflect the following points:
  - There are many ways that artists use visual recording as part of their development process. They may even use multiple forms of visual recording to achieve their outcome.
  - Some will prepare a lot of studies as a form of practice and preparation for an outcome. However, others will embark on unusual forms of recording to produce artefacts that become the outcome.

- Your selection of an artist or designer might include consideration of multiple artists and designers that use a varied approach to visual recording. This will help you to demonstrate that you are aware of how different approaches are used and will inform your work overall. For example: Rachel Whiteread is an example of an artist who uses visual recording in her development work. Whiteread continually casts objects using different materials and looks at the forms these create. These are visual records of the negative spaces that objects have. These objects become the artworks in themselves.

3 Individual responses. Reasons given should consider the process used and clearly explain how it informs your ideas.
  - Explain how the visual recording will support the technique or process you will embark on.
  - When you explain the process you might undertake in response to this, relate it back to the theme and how it links to the communication you want to achieve overall.

For example, in the extract below:

The reason I like the way this practitioner uses visual recording is that it is an unusual form of visual recording that produces a three-dimensional object.

I will inform my own development in response to this by casting helmets and objects related to protection. I could then apply colours that are associated with danger such as bright red or black and yellow hazard stripes. Alternatively, I could break the casts and this would make quite beautiful broken objects that demonstrate fragility.

Research summary (pages 19–20)
1 Individual responses, based on your research and work in relation to understanding and exploring visual recording and communication in the work of art and design practitioners, from pages 6–18.
  - When you have carried out research and gathered information, it is important to make judgements about what to use and be confident about how to inform your work.
  - Be specific about materials, techniques and processes you have seen in others' work, but refrain from copying them as your work needs to synthesise inspiration with your own responses.
  - When summarising how you will inform your development work, include consideration of form, content, process, mood and meaning.

The following example response extracts are based on the theme of 'Protection'.

When reading and interpreting the brief, my initial response to the theme and ideas was to go down the route of fragility. I saw lots of images of refugees around this time and they looked so vulnerable, especially the children. I also saw sculptures by Henry Moore and was impressed by how the forms suggested hugging, caring and protecting.

My exploration of art and design practitioners, their ideas and imagery has given me real insight into how they communicate mood through their materials. It was particularly interesting to compare Jeff Koons with Henry Moore. Koons presents brightly coloured objects like balloons that would capture the attention of children, but don't really express any of their feelings, which seem to be missing completely and much more present in Moore's forms. I like the idea of combining the two.

It was interesting to investigate and understand how contextual factors link to a theme because I knew so little about refugees and migrants around the world. While they are in the media, people in privileged countries find it hard to reconcile sharing their wealth and supporting them.

The types of visual recording I find most relevant are sketching and drawing from life models, which really appeals to me as it could help me develop a much better understanding of the human form and how its posture and composition can communicate.

Research into materials, techniques and processes led me to consider very different methods of visual recording. I was really impressed with the idea of casting as a means of visual recording when I researched Rachel Whiteread and I would like to use this for at least part of my sculpture.

The way practitioners use visual language to present a mood that I find most relevant is how Jeff Koons communicates innocence and vulnerability through the bright colour palette. The colours are highly artificial and industrial. They also give the objects they are applied to a sense of being fake and unreal. The mood this gives the audience is a feeling of being unconnected to the objects. They seem familiar, yet distant.

The formal elements in others' work that appear the most useful to my approach to the theme 'Protection' are the bright colours and surfaces that Jeff Koons creates with his sculptures. I am also interested in life-size scale sculpture that Moore uses in his murals as this enables an empathy with the object.

Non-art helped me record interesting visual forms including graphs and charts relating to wealth and inequality internationally. I saw the way Grayson Perry applies words and details to his sculptural vases and I thought I might be able to do the same.

When examining how the use of visual recording and communication informs and is applied to my own work, most of the protest work used photographic visual recording methods or illustration work that could have been traced or stencilled as a means of visual recording. It was hard to find artwork about refugees unless it was quite political work that was making a protest and I wanted to avoid that aesthetic as the processes are often very graphic, rapid and literal, which is why I am going to try casting.

The directions in which I would take a piece of art and design relating to the theme 'Protection' are to combine ideas from the colour palette of Jeff Koons, the forms of Moore and the process of Whiteread. All of these sources inspired me to make a sculptural form that looked vulnerable with another form protecting it.

Recording from primary sources (page 21)

1   Individual responses. Examples follow in relation to the theme of 'Protection'.

Recording from primary sources involves looking at real objects, places and forms to observe them directly in order to record them. For example, in relation to the theme of protection, it could mean visiting locations that may have displays of armour or weapons and using drawing and photography to observe them. Mark making can also help investigate something visually as you can print from objects, draw them from different angles and try to replicate the types of surface through the types of mark you apply.

2   Some key advantages of recording from primary sources might include the following example extracts in relation to 'Protection'. Accessing primary sources provides opportunity to observe and record from different angles. For example, I could visit the battleships in Portsmouth harbour and draw from an outside view and then draw details from inside in the cabins.

Selecting and positioning what to record is interesting because this goes beyond documentation and can actually help test whether a composition works as opposed to imagining it. Choosing to focus on the whole object or on details can radically change how that object is viewed. A hammer, for example, may look like an everyday object, but by just focusing on the claws, it could become quite menacing.

Primary sources give first-hand experience, and as individuals see things differently, each recording will be a unique interpretation, so I will try to ensure there is a balance of primary and secondary visual recording and try to access the real thing where possible.

3   Individual responses. Primary sources that could be used to explore and generate ideas in relation to 'Protection' might include any of the below, for example.

Primary source	How it can be accessed
1 Armour	I could visit a castle or museum.
2 Weapons	I could visit a clay pigeon shooting club.
3 First-aid equipment	I could talk to the college nurse and also look at what I have at home. I may have to purchase some materials from a chemist.
4 Protective clothing	It may be interesting to visit a motorbike shop and look at the protective clothing they have. I may have to talk to the owner, but if I explain it's for my art project they may be helpful.
5 People hugging or embracing	This may be tricky, but I am sure I could persuade some of my friends to model for me while I take some photos.
6 Hands and feet	I can cast my own hands and feet using modroc techniques.
7 Fences and barbed wire	This may need some long walks around town and a camera to collect lots of different views. I should avoid the main high street and look at more out-of-town areas.
8 Old, discarded children's toys	I could look in local charity shops and the local amenity tip. It may be better to bring toys home to record rather than trying to record them on location.

2D primary recording (page 22)

1–2   Individual responses. The advantage of 2D recording using different techniques and materials is to show your breadth of skill and evaluate which methods provide the most useful results. Try to take risks with materials, techniques and processes, but also try to make some considered and careful observations.

3   Individual responses. Consider the practice of doing the observation, why you tried that approach and whether it supports the overall task. In the development process, explanations should form part of your annotations in your sketchbook or development work.

Secondary sources and 2D recording (page 23)

1   Individual responses.
   • The advantage of secondary 2D recording is access to the wealth of places, objects and events that are not readily accessible to you.
   • In the development process, ensure that your exploration of visual recording is as broad as possible, so you can evaluate the most relevant materials, techniques and methods possible. You will also want to ensure that the 2D materials you make observations from are the most suitable.
   • Common mistakes are: using images that are too small and of low quality; using photographs from unhelpful angles; relying on the most obvious images that appear at the top of an internet search.

2   When explaining your choice of method and medium, you need to:
   • reference the technique you have used specifically and use the technical term if it is a traditional technique
   • link the technique or the medium to the image itself and explain how they emphasise the characteristics within the image. For example, an artist or designer may have used soft watercolours for an image that has organic properties.

Primary and secondary 3D recording (page 24)

1   Individual responses. Three different practices that would use 3D recording or communication might include:
Practice 1: Animators might make a rough model of a character to develop an awareness of how the character might move.

Practice 2: Architects will create a 3D model in CAD to get an idea of what their building will look like under different lighting conditions. This also gives them options for testing surfaces with different materials.

Practice 3: An automotive designer will make a full-scale model in clay of their car designs in order to get an accurate view of each of the creases and angles in the vehicle.

2 Individual responses. In the development process, consider how you will show that you have looked at the process different types of artist and designer might go through, and shown clearly why the process of the 3D visualisation may benefit your practice.

Camera recording with purpose (page 25)

1 Individual responses that might reflect the following points.
Method 1: I would make sure I focus the camera on specific details rather than getting quick general shots because I really want to use the different textures, surfaces and shapes within the object rather than its overall form.
Method 2: I would photograph the object under different types of light, like from the side, top and behind, in order to exaggerate the shadows and features.
Method 3: If it was a large object in a landscape, I would try to get images of it from different angles and vantage points. Together, these images would help me investigate it later and provide me with opportunities for detailed drawing studies.

2 Individual responses. Relying on a single photograph may not provide you with the most useful visual recordings for further development. The way you photograph something should enable the next stage of development.

3 When you explain or annotate the process you have used, you should be clear about how the process of photography contributes to your development. This will mean referring to the theme, but also to your plans overall. Ideally, you will emphasise the techniques you have used, such as macro, controlled lighting or use of a specific lens.

Recording through manipulation (page 26)

1 Individual responses. While predefined filters in an image manipulation program can be used here, you should not rely on these solely. In the development process, you should ensure that you work across both digital and traditional methods to show the breadth of your skills. Each example should be sufficiently different for you to make judgements that can compare the two and form the basis of your next stages of development.

Recording summary (pages 27–28)

1 Individual responses.

2 Individual responses. In the development process, it is important that your evaluations are balanced and critical about the visual recording you have done and how these have benefitted the task overall. Your evaluations should:
- be clear about how the visual recording method helps provide **insight** to an object or scene, by referring to specific formal elements
- consider the pros and cons of the materials, techniques or **processes** you have used, being able to explain overall intentions
- explain where your influences for that type of **recording** have come from by naming an artist or practice within the arts if possible
- explain how your technique sits within a wider **contextual** practice that has been used by practitioners currently or historically.

Pieces 1 and 2: Individual responses that reflect the type of annotation you would use in an actual task. You should:
- compare different techniques you have undertaken in order to find the best way forward, rather than talking about your recording in isolation
- avoid focusing simply on what you prefer doing and keep most annotation directed towards the relationship the methods have to the task and communication overall
- consider multiple opportunities for the next stages of the project and detail those steps and how they would lead into each other and benefit from the recording process.

2D and 3D ideas generation (page 29)

1–2 Individual responses.
There will be traditional methods of ideas generation used for distinct disciplines within art and design. For example, you may sketch silhouettes when fashion designing, which is a recognised form of ideas generation. It would normally be expected that you would at least try the traditional form once in your development work, so you should identify which of these are applicable to your discipline. However, you can also use methods that are more unconventional for your discipline that may provide unusual and innovative results. Your ideas generation should:
- extend your work into new territory and avoid repeating your visual recording
- try methods that are traditionally associated with your discipline, but also test alternative methods such as creating something 3D that eventually would become a 2D outcome
- take risks with ideas, materials, techniques and processes.

Experimenting to visually record (pages 30–31)

1 Individual responses. The type of surfaces you use can be diverse, but you should show knowledge of the theme that you are exploring and try to exploit a surface that has a real connection to it. Your explanations should make this clear and clarify that they were conscious choices within the development.
For example, within the theme of 'Protection':
- It might be possible to draw on a diagram of a lockable safe that you found in an old book.
- You might also simply connect the surface you work on because of its connection to the mood you want to communicate, for example a drawing that represents something of strength and defence onto a very delicate and fragile surface like rice paper.

2 Individual responses, with your choice and explanation of media being informed through your research.
- Within the development process you need to show you have considered and compared a wide range of media rather than settling with a first idea.
- Your annotation will need to show that you are aware of the issues and debates related to that specific media and also what the audience will commonly associate with that media.

3 Individual responses.
- It is really important to demonstrate that you are aware of technical methods of visualising ideas. Each discipline will have methods that are used traditionally within the discipline.
- Your annotation should explain its relevance to the discipline and how it contributes to your development overall.

Manipulating for creative intentions (page 32)

1 Individual responses, considering the following, for example:
- Explanations should introduce what you want to communicate first. This will include an outline of what you want the audience to think or experience when they see your work.
- Have a clear intention of the type of image or object you are going to present to the audience.

2 Individual responses that explain the way materials, techniques and processes will contribute to communication, specifically relating to the mood and meaning. Reasons for your choices will relate to your intentions and you will ideally:
- explain why you have selected these particular processes
- relate the materials, techniques and processes to your research and exploration in earlier stages of development.

Development summary (page 33)

1 Individual responses. Your responses at this stage in the creative process are considered as key stages and will be valuable to communicate to the audience of your work. While the research and exploration stages will have involved lots of reflection and

many creative choices, this is the point that sets off later stages of the project. Your research and investigation has broadened out, but at this point it comes together again and takes a specific path.

Your explanations for 2D and 3D ideas generation should:

- compare and contrast different types of ideas generation processes
- consider the audience, theme and your own project intentions when drawing conclusions about the ideas generation that was most suitable.

Your explanations for experimenting with diverse materials, techniques and processes should:

- emphasise how you took risks with materials, techniques and processes and assess what you learned from this
- be very specific about the materials, techniques or processes you have tried and emphasise those that were most suited to the project overall.

Your explanations for exploration through manipulating materials, techniques and processes should:

- assess how far this took you and what still has to be attempted
- review whether the exploration has benefitted the project overall and how.

Considering presentation of research (pages 34–35)

1   Individual responses that might include the types of elements from the following sample response extracts:
    Method 1: I could photograph my work and sketchbook pages and use Photoshop to organise the information. The benefits of doing this would be that I could easily make changes to the layout at later stages if I want to rearrange or add anything. Having images of the sketchbook would also show the way I record and develop.
    Method 2: I could create a set grid design and apply it to all of the sheets. This will make it easy to lay out and give them a uniform approach. The organisation and structuring of this will need to allow enough images to show the breadth of work I have done, but only focus on the most important elements.
    Method 3: I could lay out all of the pieces I have worked on using a white surface background and then photograph them using a good camera. These could then become the actual pages I display. I may need to touch up the brightness and contrast and also add some writing later to help communicate the different elements.

2   Individual responses. Your responses should, for example:

- show that you have considered alternative approaches and reflected on which is the most suited to your work and creative process
- include some discussion of selection as you will not be able to show absolutely everything you have done
- clarify how each sheet will represent a specific part of the creative process.

3–4   Individual responses. Your layouts should, for example:

- show an understanding of grid structures, margins and columns
- show some consistency of layout between the sheets
- identify key parts such as titles, areas for images and distinct areas for text
- keep a clear and simple layout in order to help the audience understand your work
- include a chronological structure and outline how this may progress on the specific page, i.e. left to right, top to bottom, clockwise, and so on.

Producing art or design (pages 36–37)

1   Individual responses. Consider the points below in relation to your outline, for example.

- It may not be completely detailed, but should give a good idea of the materials, techniques and processes you would propose to use and the form it would take.

- It should justify your choices of direction based on your research and development so far.
- It should avoid making radical departures from the development work undertaken, but may be more ambitious in scope.
- Explain how visual recording has supported your project overall and influenced your methods of visually communicating.

2   Individual responses, considering the points below, for example.

(a)   You need to be confident that the interpretation of the imagery will be well recognised as relating to the theme and have some logical connection to it.

(b)   You may have multiple contextual influences on your work, but you should describe the most pertinent.

(c)   You should explain how you are confident your manipulation of materials, techniques and processes are the most suitable methods and justify your choices.

3   Individual responses. Your visualisations in your actual project can be done in any media that is relevant to the discipline in which you are working. There may also be multiples with subtle variants.

4   Individual responses.

- It is important to be confident about your choices and give good reasons for them.
- Avoid responses that: state that you are using it simply because another artist has; show that another preferred technique may be better, but you have not opted for it because others may be easier; jump to a new material, technique or process because nothing else seems to have worked.

Applying skills for creative intentions (pages 38–39)

1   Individual responses. At this point you should show that you have a good awareness of who your potential audience is and who you want to communicate to. In your responses you should:

- describe who the audience is using terminology related to demographics. You should show that you are familiar with what your audience normally expects from artwork or products that have been created in the past or that they are accustomed to. You will have a clear idea of what this will do for the audience and how it will enable them to relate to the work.
- discuss visual language that is widely recognised in contemporary society. This might be by connecting it to wider popular cultural imagery that is synonymous with a type of communication. You should name these directly and explain why your work borrows from that area.

2   Individual responses. You can take risks with how you apply your work to products, but try to have logical reasons for where and how you apply it in order to give it purpose. It may not work straight away. You may want to start with literal options first and test how these function, before selecting the best option. You should show that you are aware of how art and design work can be applied for a purpose. This might be creating an illustration for a magazine cover or a fabric for a garment.

Considering presentation factors (pages 40–41)

1   Individual responses. An example response extract follows:
    I can demonstrate the small details of the work by showing the whole image quite large on the page, but then including close-up pictures of important details underneath it.
    I can clarify the materials used in the work by using clearly labelled swatches with the material. I could draw lines from the materials to the outcome itself to be really clear.
    I can clarify the process used in the creative process by making it really clear using labels that my work went through specific stages. I could number them and put a title, such as 'Process stage 1' and so on, next to the images.
    For time-based work, I could clarify the length by outlining the medium and having key scenes or images from the work in a line. I would then need to clearly label the duration next to these.

2   Individual responses. Your responses should, for example:
   - be clear about the audience for the work
   - identify other work like your own and how it has been presented
   - explain the visual language and what formats and media would suit this discipline and practice
   - identify the type of written work to be placed on the pages, its clarity, scale, length and scope.

3

Questions	Example 1	Example 2	Example 3
Which of the three has the least text information on the scale and materials?		✓	
Which clarifies the scale, media and technical information the most?			✓
Which has the least information, visual or text, about the scale and media of the outcome?	✓		
Which of the three may confuse the viewer as to the outcome?	✓		✓
Which of the three seems to include development work?	✓		

4   Individual responses. It is important that you justify your reasons and don't just rely on the fact that you prefer certain formats. Some of the reasons you give may include the following, for example:
   - Including the object being held or in use gives a real sense of scale and demonstrates how that object performs in real life.
   - Having clear, bold writing with a title and some quick details about the work helps people understand what they are looking at.
   - Showing the development work on a page with the outcome really helps place it within the overall process of development.
   - One large picture with some close-up details means the viewer can see the full image, but can also appreciate some of the craftsmanship within the image.
   - It may not be possible to have an image of large-scale work that enables the viewer to see the materials.
   - Having a bold title for the work can help express what the communication intentions were.
   - Too many images that overlap can be confusing for the viewer and it may be better to stick to a grid.
   - Including some detail of the process such as mark making means the viewer will appreciate the type of craftsmanship involved.
   - Short introductions to the project purpose help contextualise the visuals.
   - Layering of images using transparency within the development work enables the communication of a development process.
   - Images from lots of angles, especially for a functional object, give a real insight into how something works.

Considering presentation of final piece (page 42)
1   Individual responses. You will want to draw the audience's attention to particular qualities in your work. You can do this in the following ways, for example:

Response to the theme	• Creating a title that connects clearly to the original theme in the brief.
	• Having a short description of how your work connects to the theme.
	• Highlighting any key parts of the process or work that most closely relate to the theme.
Manipulation of materials, techniques and processes	• Having close-up images of important materials, techniques and processes.
	• Indicating how your materials, techniques or processes connect to historic or contextually relevant practices.
	• Including written details of important materials, techniques or processes.

2   Individual responses. Your presentation of the outcome will, for example:
   - acknowledge the audience and their needs
   - balance your own personal preferences with those of others
   - try to emphasise the work rather than a wish to be creative with the presentation
   - consider grounds or background that will be neutral and help emphasise the work
   - try to communicate the functionality or traits of the work.

Commentary on research (page 43)
Your answers to this section need to:
   - use technical terminology where possible
   - show a range of methods you have employed
   - acknowledge the importance of recording from both primary and secondary sources
   - explain a connection that the methods had with the theme
   - demonstrate that the process was beneficial to generating ideas.
1   Individual responses.
2   Four things that could be improved are the following, for example:
   (a) The commentary suggests the writer isn't really interested in visual recording.
   (b) The learner assumes that photography is better than drawing, without explaining why.
   (c) There is no justification for relying on camouflage apart from personal preference.
   (d) There is an over-reliance on Google Images and a dismissal of primary research.
3   When comparing extracts and noting improvements, you might notice the following, for example:
   - The writer immediately references the influences other practitioners have had on them and shows awareness of how others record.
   - The writer tries to positively record from primary sources where possible and uses creative ways of accessing these.
   - The writer clearly connects camouflage to the overall theme of protection in a relevant way.
   - The writer discusses the importance of using different materials, techniques and processes along with a broad range of sources.

Commentary on ideas generation (page 44)
1   Individual responses that might include the following, for example:
   - You can comment on ideas generation processes as these may have been experimental and unconventional and others may be interested in your methods.
   - They may give insight into why your project has resulted in the outcomes you are presenting.
   - The methods you employed may have been influenced by a practitioner or movement and this could have a bearing on what it is communicating.

2. Ideas generation processes might include, among others:
   - mind maps
   - observing
   - synthesis
   - mood boards
   - juxtaposition
   - deconstruction
   - drawing
   - layering
   - connection.
3. Individual responses. Consider the following points:
   - You should emphasise the importance of ideas generation techniques, use technical terminology where possible and show that you were willing to take risks within that process.
   - You should avoid any suggestion that you had already made up your mind about what the outcome was going to be as this will suggest that you were not going to benefit from the ideas generation process.

Commentary on formal elements (page 45)

1. Individual responses. You should use the technical terms for formal elements including line, tone, form, texture, colour, pattern, scale, perspective, figure and ground or composition.
2. Individual responses. You should list at least three of the formal elements, but your answers may justify the use of them in combination. You should explain how the formal elements emphasise certain qualities in the work and how you intend the audience to experience it.
3.

Analysis of extracts	Extract 1	Extract 2
Which relates the theme to the formal elements used?	✓	
Which doesn't connect the formal elements to the communication intentions?		✓
Which objectively discusses the communication intentions?	✓	
Which makes bold statements about the audience's needs?		✓
Which suggests learning from others?	✓	

Commentary on Ms, Ts and Ps (page 46)

1.

Analysis of extracts	Extract	Explanation
Which statement contextualises the use of materials most?	B	
Which makes assumptions about the audience, rather than giving a balanced point of view?	A	
Which of the commentaries focuses most on the future instead of the project?	C	While it is useful to discuss future intentions, this should not be the central justification of the answer.
Which relates the process of production most to the communication intentions?	D	
Which relates most to relevant principles for the unit?	D	Drawing is discussed within the writing and there is a clear explanation of how ideas have evolved.
Which discusses process as a valid principle for creating the product?	D	

2. Individual responses.

Commentary on creative decisions (pages 47–48)

1.

Statement	Tick	Explanation
Artists and designers make decisions based on instinct alone.		Some decisions may come from instinct, but there will be a process of trial and error which will support evaluation. This will lead to creative decisions.
Artists and designers make creative decisions based on what they are trying to communicate.	✓	
Artists and designers want to make beautiful things and this is the guiding principle.		Beauty can be an important principle, but there is no fixed notion of what beauty is and it can be dangerous to assume that something is beautiful for everyone.
Some solutions to creative problems are solved through trial and error.	✓	
Artists and designers should be free to use materials, techniques and processes however they want.		Creative freedom is important, but constraints and audience or user needs are equally important.
Artists and designers use evaluation to work through a process of improvement.	✓	
Artists and designers can learn about the appropriateness of materials, techniques and processes used by others.	✓	
All observation should focus on what other artists and designers have done.		It is possible to rely too heavily on influences by others. While it is important to look at what others have done, you will also need to present your own personal observations in order to innovate.

2. Individual responses.
3. (a) Because they found that it was not reflecting the properties of strength they wanted to communicate. They also realised that wider contextual research may prove more beneficial to their communication intentions.
   (b) The learner realises there is a great opportunity to include the strength qualities of eggs within the visual communication of the packaging. They also make a conscious decision to move away from the early visual recording with eggs towards more scientific experiments. They discuss each of the stages and explain how each relates to the next stage.
   (c) The learner knows that their work has to stand out from other products in the market and that it will have to compete for the attention of the consumer in the supermarket.
   (d) A range of testing is discussed and some of these tests are quite experimental. While the learner wasn't always sure that the experiments would be beneficial, they attempted them in order to identify their potential.
   (e) Two different ways the learner might have researched this issue:
      - They could have analysed a range of packaging prior to embarking on experimentation.
      - They could have undertaken a survey of what the audience liked about different types of packaging.

Commentary on purpose, meaning and intent (page 49)

1 Individual responses that list key influences on your work. You may put these in order of significance. It is always important to explain how these key pieces of information combined to generate an impact. The pieces of information should demonstrate more than common knowledge and reflect the research you put into developing your project.

2 While not all of the bullets will be central to your work, it is important to indicate how each contributes and to what extent. You should explain the relevance of each and potentially compare it with alternatives that you considered.

3 Your answers should be balanced and show an honest critique of your work. Some points to consider are shown below, for example.

One strength with what it communicates is:	The reason I think this is because:
• it may be very clear to the audience • it may provoke valuable reactions from the audience • it may present an innovative approach to the theme.	• you should be able to connect these issues to the formal elements within the work • you could attribute this to a stage in the creative process • you could explain how you propose to capitalise on this learning in the future.
An issue with what the work communicates is:	The reason I think this is because:
• it may be quite vague and unclear for the audience • it may send mixed or even conflicting messages to the audience • it may be too didactic in what it is trying to communicate.	• you should be able to connect these issues to the formal elements within the work • you could attribute this to a stage in the creative process • you could potentially offer solutions here.

Writing a focused commentary (page 50)

1 Individual responses, considering the factors below, for example. While many people will see the creative process as being linear, it may be that your work goes back and forth between recording, research, experimentation and refinement. During this time, there will be specific reasons why you had to switch practices. For example, you may have got stuck with refinement, because a particular technique wasn't providing a suitable finish. This may have resulted in you doing further ideas generation. You won't be able to talk about all of these stages, but need to evaluate which points were the most important and resulted in the most significant advances and innovation in the work.

1	My starting point – using primary and secondary visual research	2	Key development decisions I took along the way
3	Benefits of specific experiments	4	Use of visual recording within the ideas generation
5	Benefits of visual recording to the outcome	6	Visual recording and communication techniques employed

2 Solutions to issues to help write a strong commentary:

Issue: Being overly subjective and using personal opinions Solution: Include balanced judgements and justify your opinions.	Issue: Assuming the reader knows me and my project Solution: Include a short introduction, frame the project, the audience and intentions.
Issue: Not covering all of the important points Solution: Make a list of what to cover and give your commentary structure.	Issue: Repetition and overuse of specific words Solution: Use a thesaurus or synonyms tool and proofread what you have written.
Issue: Not having an ending Solution: Write a conclusion that includes what you would do for improvement.	Issue: Saying everything is perfect Solution: Balance the issues with the work with the positive aspects.

3 Individual responses. Keeping to the point with writing is important. Where possible, see whether short sentences might be combined using a comma or conjunction. You want to keep the overall meaning, but proofread what you have written and see whether pieces can be left out. An example response extract follows:

As a solution to early confusion, the creative process required a combination of research into relevant artists and non-art contextual information. My skills and knowledge have improved through exploiting new subjects and intensive artist research and exploration of materials and techniques. Importantly, I now follow ideas until I achieve a product and results. I have also learned graphic methods of metaphor and representation that support the visualisation of my ideas.

Revision activities

Revision activity 1 (page 51)

Individual responses that should be assessed against the criteria noted.

While the following are just examples and there is room for some variation, these cover key elements and may be a useful order to consider:

Presentation sheet 1	Presentation sheet 2	Presentation sheet 3
• Initial research into visual recording and communication by others • Ideas generation • Mind maps • Mood board • Sketches and drawings of ideas • Details of primary and secondary sources	• Testing and exploration of visual recording • Testing and exploration of visual communication • Traditional and unconventional recording • Primary and secondary recording • At least two ideas explored	• Major experiments • Materials and swatches • Draft outcomes such as prototypes, models, tests, rough, mock-up, render, alpha, toile • Testing and refinement

Revision activity 2 (page 52)

Individual responses that should be assessed against the criteria noted and demonstrate the following:

- Your response to a theme – including title and some writing about how it connects to the brief. Ideally use the same word as the theme set in the brief. If the object itself isn't clear, use diagrams or information to explain it to the audience. This is especially true if the work is not immediately evident.
- Your use of materials, techniques and processes – including swatches of materials or close-up images of specific details in the work. You can use lines or information to indicate how these

are used in the outcome, especially if it is 3D. If the work went through a process, you may want to show some small images of the different stages. If the technique is important, you can state what these were using technical vocabulary.

- Your ability to communicate your creative intentions – clarify what your intentions were. If the work has been created for a specific product or audience, make sure this is clear on the sheet. Where the work is a fine art piece, your intentions may have been to provoke specific questions in the viewer. Products and design pieces can simulate or demonstrate how they would be used.

Revision activity 3 (page 53)

Individual responses that should be assessed against the criteria noted.

You can use the following prompts as a guide to your commentary. You may have more to say about certain stages than others, but you should try to cover as many as possible. Always justify your points and accurately use technical and visual vocabulary.

• Your interpretation of a theme	• Discuss what your first reactions were. • Explain why you interpreted the theme and how this was a relevant path to follow.
• The art and design practitioners you researched and how they influenced your work	• Include specific names of practitioners, art movements and their methods of visual recording. • Include specific names of practitioners, art movements and their methods of visual communication. • Make reference to materials, techniques and processes, mood, meaning and formal elements.
• The primary and secondary sources you used in response to a theme	• Discuss and compare primary and secondary. • Indicate the lengths you were willing to go to, to ensure you benefitted from visual recording.
• The visual recording methods and material you used	• Explain the influences the methods you used had on your development process. • Explain how the visual records impacted on later stages of the project.
• Your own visual recording and communication in relation to a theme	• Outline the visual language you have started to develop. • Explain how it relates to the theme and the audience.
• Key decisions made	• Underline the major hurdles you had to overcome and what decisions you took to resolve them. • Justify your points with logical and objective arguments where possible.
• Strengths and weaknesses and areas for improvement in your own work	• List the strengths and weaknesses within the work. • Outline which stage of the creative process impacted on the strengths and weaknesses. • Indicate how you could improve the work, focusing on stages of the creative process, refinement and visual recording and communication.

Unit 2: Critical and Contextual Studies in Art and Design

Planning an investigation (page 61)

1 Individual responses. Additional factors might include, for example:
- primary sources such as visits to galleries, museums, studios or workshops
- secondary sources such as the internet, journals, books, publications
- sources of contextual factors that influenced the practitioners/their work such as the time or era that work was produced, or any political, social and cultural influences. These may include technological and scientific.

2 Individual responses. The following kind of points might be included, for example:
- Intention: In this contextual investigation, I am researching the theme of illusion and how it features in the work of M.C. Escher and David Hockney.
- Clear aims: I want to find out how Surrealism and perspective is used as a device to create the illusion of space in artwork, by looking at M.C. Escher's and David Hockney's work.
- Clear objectives: I will research from primary sources by visiting a gallery that has examples of both Surrealist paintings and drawings, and some of Hockney's work, making drawings from the works, and taking photographs if permitted.
- I will research from secondary sources by using books, journals and the reputable internet – I will be studying examples of Escher's work, and considering if and how he adopts Surrealistic devices; I will look at Hockney's drawings that explored perspective and research into their ideas and writings.
- I will research contextual influences by finding out if the artists were influenced by illusion in Surrealist works, and in ideas about representing the illusion of space, as well as any other specific influences on their work.
- Timescale and action plans (specific, measurable, achievable, realistic and time-related): I will make my off-site visits in the first two weeks, and combine these with library sessions; I will collate information and review in week three, and undertake further research and consolidate the research to form conclusions from week four on.
- Methods to record and collate findings and bibliography: I will use drawings and photographs. I may also explore actual drawings and photography of my own subjects that show perspective and the illusion of space. I will use a sketchbook to collate information, annotate research, propose actions and use the Harvard system to reference books and sources.

Using annotation (pages 62–63)

1 Individual responses for annotation that might include the following points, for example:
- The image shows the repetition of the public face of this movie star and celebrity, creating a feeling of over-exposure, like TV screens all playing the same picture.
- The image is an example of Warhol taking subject matter from popular culture and the media.
- Each image has a subtle difference in the way the overprinted facial features have actually been printed – Warhol allows imperfections in the printmaking process to show through.
- Warhol's technique of allowing the materials, techniques and processes used in the image to break down can suggest the same might happen for this artificial persona that was created by the studio and the film industry publicity machine.
- Readings of the image have suggested it is almost showing the way Monroe has faded away – literally, as the printing suggests – leaving behind a trace image.
- The colours appear unnatural and striking, and combine to create the instantly recognisable iconography of the Marilyn Monroe image.

2   Individual responses using annotation to briefly record initial visual analysis of a piece of work, deconstructing through formal elements, visual language and visual communication.

Organising your notes (page 64)

1   Individual responses. Ways of organising your notes and why might include the following points, for example:
    Headings and key points:
    - The theme – including definition and how it is used in work researched, what caused it to be used as a theme, what contextual factors influenced its development.
    - Practitioner A – how they use the theme, and how they use materials, techniques and processes, how they were influenced by specific contextual factors.
    - Practitioner B – how they use the theme, and how they use materials, techniques and processes, how they were influenced by specific contextual factors.
    - Contextual factors – key developments that were influencing art and design in the periods the practitioners were working in.
    Cross-referencing work by:
    - making links between the research gathered for each practitioner and the research on contextual factors in the periods they were working
    - making links between the way the theme is expressed in practitioners' work, and how they use materials, techniques and processes.

2   Example sources styled using a recognised reference system – example references below using the Harvard system.
    Style for books: Phaidon Editors & Melick, T. (2014) *The Art Book: Mini Format*. London: Phaidon Press.
    Style for journal articles: Badhurst, M. (2016) Designing Functionality. *Aesthetica, The Art and Culture Magazine*, Issue 70, pp.94–98.
    Style for websites: Museum of Modern Art (MoMA) (2017) Adams, A. (1933) *New Mexico*, gelatin silver print, 18.4cm × 24.1cm. Photography (image) [online] Available at: www.moma.org/collection/works/44000?locale=en [Accessed 28 October 2017].
    Style for bibliography: uses the same format as a reference list but includes everything read about the topic, not only the sources mentioned in written work, presented in alphabetical order by surname.
    Style for primary sources: e.g. drawing/photo/notes: *Matisse Exhibition*, Royal Academy of Arts, London, November 2017.

3   Individual responses. Ways of regularly recording personal thoughts and reflections might include, for example, reviewing research progress each week and summarising findings on, for instance, what has been learned about a theme, or findings on this and its relationship to the work of practitioners, and how it is manifested in specific examples of their work.

Writing for scenarios (pages 65–66)

1   Individual responses to selected questions. These might include the factors in the example extracts that follow.
    - The purpose of an exhibition catalogue is to provide information on the exhibitor(s), including biographical details and images in a sequence or by category. The catalogue is used to explain the practitioner's work in terms of the exhibition theme, contextual influences and relevant criticism.
    - The language choice will be third person, for example 'Graphic designers, animators and filmmakers use illusion throughout their work to convince, cajole and inspire their audiences in a variety of ways'. When considering whether the style should be formal or informal, think about the intended audience and readers. The language should be accessible and clear without being oversimple or uninformative, and should use the appropriate tone.
    - The audience might include specialists and non-specialists, so it will be important to use appropriate terminology with explanations if required. Images can be used to show a visible example of a specialist technique or process.

- Some catalogue entries have a limit of, for example, around 1800 words, so it is important to write clearly and edit to avoid repetition. Use phrases concisely and reference other chapters/areas where appropriate.
- I will use headings to give a logical structure to the catalogue entry and ensure a balance of text and visuals so that there is a focus of information on specific aspects of the exhibition such as theme and contextual influences, including images that highlight specific aspects or treatments of the theme.

> Ask your tutor or check the latest Sample Assessment Material on the Pearson website to establish what is required in your actual assessment and whether there is a word limit for any activities. Assessment detail may change so always make sure you are up to date.

2   Individual responses. Initial thoughts for an introductory paragraph for an exhibition catalogue might include the following points, for example:
    - Introduce the theme, with definition.
    - Introduce practitioners, with a sentence explaining how they use or represent the theme in their work.
    - Briefly explain any links between their approaches to the theme – how similar are they, and how different are they?
    - Create interest by making links between their work and subsequent interest and influences they have had on other practitioners.
    - Relate their work to any specific wider contextual factors to create further interest.
    - Define the timespan of the practitioners' careers the show could cover, such as a sequential journey through a period of their work, or an examination of key works that show treatments of the theme.

Writing justifications (pages 67–68)

1–3   Individual responses reflecting the chosen practitioner, work and theme.

4   Individual responses. Initial thoughts for the concluding paragraph of the letter in the scenario might include, for example:
    - initial sentence that explains the conclusion, by stating the practitioner who should appear first
    - following sentences that state the thinking behind this conclusion
    - points that form the justification should include:
      ○ the way the chosen practitioner's work exemplifies and communicates the theme in the strongest or clearest way
      ○ the depth in which they have studied or explored this theme
      ○ how they have explored different ways of showing the theme, so their work remains interesting
      ○ audience reaction to their work, public and professional
    - further sentences comparing the chosen practitioner's work to those practitioners considered less fitting to lead the show. The points used to justify the chosen practitioner's work should be directly addressed in the comparisons
    - explanations of how the sequence of the exhibition could be used to provide a narrative for the audience on the theme and the different ways practitioners attempt to communicate it
    - explanations on how other areas such as contextual factors and influence on other practitioners can be included in the exhibition.

Considering themes and ideas (page 69)

1–2   Individual responses reflecting the chosen practitioners, themes and ideas.

Understanding contextual influences (pages 70–72)

1–4 Individual responses.

For example, contextual influences on *Meshes*, Michael Brennand-Wood, might include the following:

- 20th-century modernism – Agnes Martin, Kazimir Malevich. (Search on the West Dean visual arts site for information on the visiting artist Michael Brennand-Wood.)
- Polyrhythmic compositions structures in music – John Cage, Steve Reich, Philip Glass, Terry Riley.
- Eastern decorative traditions – in textiles, in Islamic calligraphy.
- Synthesis of traditional and contemporary materials, and historical and contemporary sources. (Search on the Michael Brennand-Wood website and select 'Michael'.)
- Social – early family life, father engineer, mother industrial weaver. (Search on the 'Ideas in the Making' website (www.themaking.org.uk) for Michael Brennand-Wood, Maker of the month, February 2011.)

For example, contextual influences on *Untitled*, Ian Davenport, might include the following:

- Contemporary colour palettes used in 2D animation/TV – *The Simpsons*. (Search for *The Guardian* article 'Artist Ian Davenport launches Colourfall, his first UK retrospective' (10.6.14).)
- Colour palettes in old master paintings – Hans Holbein's *The Ambassadors*; colour palette used by Vincent van Gogh.
- Colour theory and how the audience perceives colour. (Search for the Ian Davenport video clip: 'The making of Giardini Colourfall and Wide Acres of Time'.)
- Drumming/percussion – using colour in rhythmic sense in own work. (Search for the Ian Davenport video clip 'The making of Giardini Colourfall and Wide Acres of Time'.)
- Science, in how gravity affects poured paint, and influences the physical nature of final artworks. (Search 'BBC, Where I live, Coventry and Warwickshire, Ian Davenport painting walls at uni'.)

5 Individual responses. The example extract summaries below reflect some key contextual influences on the practitioners' works on pages 70–71.

Meshes – Michael Brennand-Wood

20th-century modernism influenced Brennand-Wood to create designs that explored geometrical forms, as he had been inspired by the suprematist paintings of Kazimir Malevich. However, this influence is tempered by the duality that exists in Brennand-Wood's work. The suprematists' influence is absorbed, redefined, and made softer in in the grid-like structures in *Meshes* due to the way materials have been used. Brennand-Wood's use of materials is directly influenced by his social background. His mother was an industrial weaver, and his father was an engineer and used wood and metal to make items that interested Brennand-Wood. These influences translate into the wooden structures and supports of his pieces, and the woven nature of materials. Sometimes he fuses – literally – traditional and modern materials. His use of motif in *Meshes* references Eastern decorative traditions in its pattern. Brennand-Wood uses colour and shape in repetition and in a structural density that is influenced by musical compositions. These are notably those that apply a rhythm-based repetitive system to evolve into a final piece. The repetition of shapes and structures in his work, woven together in open networks, is one way his work shows this influence.

Untitled – Ian Davenport

Ian Davenport's work is essentially about colour. He controls colour, or allows it to become something else, through exploiting the inherent quality of the materials – its viscosity – to make unpredictability part of his working method. He uses gravity as a tool in his making techniques, allowing the paint to run in controlled lines and then pool at the base of the work. His colour use reflects his interest in the colourways and combinations across a wide range of sources. These range from old master paintings, for example those of Hans Holbein and Van Gogh,

to contemporary work on TV and 2D digital animation. This interest is linked to his continuing theme of how the audience sees colour, and how he can use colour to try to reference the world. He is also interested in the rhythm in drumming, and used a drum kit in his studio as part of his working practice. He has explained how he is interested in the way colour can create a sort of rhythm in the lines flowing down the work's surface, and how this changes as they distort in the pooling at the bottom. Many other artists have explored the links between aspects of music and painting such as Paul Klee, and in this way, Davenport is continuing a tradition in abstract painting.

Investigating key works (page 73)

1 Individual responses.

2 Individual responses.

For example, a key work chosen for Bridget Riley might be *Fall*, 1963, polyvinyl acetate paint on hardboard, 1410 mm × 1403 mm, which can be found on the Tate Gallery website.

This may be chosen as a key work for the following reasons:

- Riley's use of black and white and how it can be used optically, such as in patterns where it can give the illusion of additional colours and/or tones.
- Riley's use of rhythm as a key component in her work.
- A key characteristic in op art is the way the positioning of lines, curves and visual elements can create the impression of movement, of compression, of space and depth.
- Riley's use of a pure colour or monochromatic palette to represent her sensations and communicate without any specific reference to external objects or motifs.
- The development of Riley's own personal journey from motif to abstraction – as in her work inspired by Seurat, which further developed Riley's interest and fascination with colour and optical mixing (see optical mixing in Seurat).
- *Fall* shows how the illusion of compression and movement can be achieved in an abstracted format.

Deconstructing formal elements (page 74)

1 Individual responses depending on the practitioner and selected key work and the use of formal elements.

For example, formal elements used in Bridget Riley's *Fall*:

- line
- pattern
- colour/tonal values (monochrome)
- shape.

2 Individual responses depending on practitioner. Sample response extract for Bridget Riley's *Fall*, for example:

- Line is used to create the flowing pattern, which in turn creates the rhythm in the piece.
- This is arranged in a square shape or format, and allows the image to focus the viewer on the symmetrical nature of the work.
- There is more space between the curves in the upper half of the piece, and then these become compressed in the lower half, creating an effect of compressed space and movement.
- This movement may reflect the title *Fall*, as the piece may show space falling away.
- The ability in painting and the potential in lines and patterns to suggest movement is a key characteristic of Optical Art – Riley was associated with this movement.
- Although Riley uses a monochrome palette, its contrast of black and white can act on the audience's perception to suggest other tones and in some cases colours – again, this reinforces the theme of illusion, and was exploited by other artists such as Victor Vasarely and Josef Albers.

Deconstructing visual language (pages 75–76)

1 Individual responses.

For example, some key points about visual language used in Bridget Riley's *Fall* might include:

- composition: the image is square, not a traditional portrait or landscape format. This composition also focuses the viewer on the regularity of the piece. The square format was also used extensively by other artists who were exploring the potential in colour-led abstraction and pattern work – Albers and Vasarely, for example.

- materials: Riley has made the work using polyvinyl acetate paint on hardboard. This is an alternative medium to the more traditional oil on canvas or board.
- process: the way this work has been made is key to its visual language. The paint is a stripped-down set of lines and spaces, arranged and described in such a way that they create the illusion of movement, space and rhythm.
- production methods: the reduction of the process of painting to creating stripes in acetate-based medium is a key direction in the work, and means that its formal values are part of its visual language – there is no motif or iconography for the viewer to read or deconstruct its symbolism. The painting can be seen and felt directly. Riley was not concerned with her work being read in a narrative or illustrational sense.
- sources: Tate Gallery, Bridget Riley, [online] Available at: www.tate.org.uk/art/artists/bridget-riley-1845 [Accessed 27 October 2017].

2 Individual responses depending on chosen piece of art and design.

Deconstructing visual communication (page 77)

1 Individual responses.

In relation to Bridget Riley, considerations might include the points below, from sample response extracts.

(a) Visual communication to highlight a theme in a work:
Riley has used visual communication as a way of showing audiences that colour or monochrome can be used to create works that are free from any specific illustrational or narrative role. Instead, they are able to create the illusion of movement, depth and space through the way the viewer receives and perceives the carefully controlled line and formal elements. In this way, she is continuing and extending the development of the scientific interest that one of the artists that inspired her was also experimenting with: Georges Seurat had been inspired by science in optical colour mixing, and Riley has continued this in the way she uses tonal (monochrome) elements to create the illusion of other colours and/or tones. Her use of polyvinyl acetate marks her work as different from the traditional oil on canvas route, even when the artists were working in abstract terms. Technology had enabled paints and new materials to become more widely available. Her work could be said to represent something of the modern times when it was made.

(b) Visual communication to communicate message(s) or meaning(s):
Riley's work points to the idea of the painting being of itself and not having to reference any particular scene or object. This is a message that some modernist art of the 20th century had been developing towards, by slowly replacing purely figurative recording with a systematic abstraction and distillation of the image into its purest component parts. Riley has not included any subject matter or obvious visual clue to the work being a picture of something. Instead, she is showing the viewer the potential of colour and tone (monochrome) to be a subject in its own right, and is controlling this by the way she is using formal elements and visual language. It is also communicating an idea about the way paintings can affect the audience. This may be in the way artworks may contain messages that need to be interpreted. This was a developing idea in many artists' work at this time – it was felt painting could become about painting itself. The painting is an image that is open to interpretation, and so encourages the audience to become involved by reading it.

Summarising key information (pages 78–79)

1 Individual responses depending on the practitioner and key piece of art and design.

Making connections (page 80)

1 Individual responses that should consider the following points. Similarities and differences in how the practitioners:
- use formal elements, such as line, colour, tonal values
- use visual language – for example, in Riley's work, pattern and rhythm, or in Escher's work, control of positive and negative space and interlocking shapes
- use visual communication – such as in the message in their work, their use of any subject matter
- use subject matter or imagery in their work
- use media and materials in the making and production phases in their work – such as Riley's use of polyvinyl acetate
- use techniques and processes in making their work – such as Davenport's use of a syringe to control paint
- are influenced by contextual factors, such as technology, or science, or social factors, such as the work of other practitioners in Riley's work.

2 Individual responses that should consider the following points:
- How the key work exemplifies some of the ideas in the practitioner's work, such as Riley's *Fall* showing her preoccupations with the release from depicting a subject.
- How this work shows the theme and how this example may best exemplify this, as in Riley's *Fall* creating the illusion of movement and shifting space.
- If the work gave the practitioner a focus on their working output, or represented a turning point for them, such as being considered important by critics, or being showcased in an important exhibition or event.
- Whether the work was critically received as a defining point, where the practitioner had crystallised their ideas and the theme.
- How the work demonstrates the visual characteristics and identity of the practitioner's work, such as being open to different readings as in Riley's *Fall*. Interestingly, she wrote for a catalogue of paintings being shown in 1964 that she found it 'difficult to make a comment concerning *Fall* … because it is a recent work that gives rise to certain possibilities I intend to develop in future paintings … to make a conclusive statement' (Chamot, M., Farr, D. & Butlin, M. (1964) *The Modern British Paintings, Drawings and Sculpture* Issue 1, Artists A–L. London: The Oldbourne Press).
- If the work exerted any influence on other practitioners.

Making comparisons and links (page 81)

1 Individual responses.
For example:
- Define the theme and explain how each practitioner shows this in their work, such as in the illusion of interlocking shapes morphing from fish to bird and back again in the Escher example.
- Use analysis from making connections pages to highlight links and similarities in their work, such as Escher's use of shape and Riley's use of tone with a monochrome pattern depicting a kind of movement.
- Use this to confirm and state which best shows the theme.

2 Individual responses.
For example:
- Refer directly to the theme, comparing and contrasting the examples of work in more detail, such as the Escher and Riley images in relation to the theme of 'Illusion'.
- Refer to the way in which the message is communicated, for example which practitioner does this in the most direct way?
- Refer directly to the theme, comparing the example of work to support the argument you are developing.
- Use this to confirm and support your justification on which best shows the theme and should lead in the exhibition catalogue.

1 Individual responses that might reflect the following points, for example.

Aspects to consider when forming and justifying conclusions and judgements in relation to copy to be included in an exhibition catalogue:

- Defining the theme and explaining how each practitioner has addressed it in their visual work, such as subject matter.
- Comparing and contrasting the work of each practitioner in a succinct manner, highlighting any key contextual influences on their work, such as the work of others, technology, and so on.
- Summarising information and conclusions, with appropriate terminology, such as when describing formal elements and visual language.

Key aspects to consider when putting forward a balanced argument with justification for opinions and conclusions in relation to who should appear at the start of the catalogue:

- Explaining how you have identified the practitioner that best exemplifies the theme in their work, such as analysing their work.
- Noting any defining key works that could be said to represent the theme in a way that has influenced others, or been accepted as a key work that defines the theme.
- Including supporting statements or views found as part of research, such as in other exhibition catalogues or in reviews.

When making justifications, it is important to support them by including/using:

- relevant quotations, such as critical writings, practitioner's own quotations
- visual analysis, such as using specific examples to highlight and justify a point
- references and bibliography, such as the work of others if appropriate, such as describing the influence of work on others if considered key.

2 Individual responses.

Revision activities

Revision activity 1 (pages 83–84)

Individual responses that should be assessed against the criteria noted.

Revision activity 2 (page 85)

Individual responses that should be assessed against the criteria noted.

Unit 6: Managing a Client Brief

Responding to the brief (pages 99–100)

1 Individual responses to summarise requirements of the revision task brief that might include the points below, for example:

- The brief is based on visual identity in materials and staff, as part of a brand development process.
- The design should embody information and support if possible or appropriate, as these are key aspects of the client's identity and function.
- The organisation relies on fundraising for its income.
- The design is targeting young people aged 11–18 years and young adults aged 19–34 years – this brief requires one of these to be selected.
- The brief requires one of the big issues to be selected and included as a driver for the design work.
- One brief has to be selected, and ideas and research developed based on this.
- An ongoing log needs to be maintained, showing records and notes of the development.
- This has to be progressed through to a final design idea, and used for a presentation.

- Speaker notes need to be produced to accompany this.

2 Individual responses to summarise the revision task information that might include the points below, for example:

- Have to analyse and extract key points from the information on the client. This will provide information on the specific requirements and direction for the work.
- Have to select one of the big issues to include as a focus for the project.
- The client information will contain prompts as to the content that practical work will need to address, through identifying themes, key points, and so on.
- Required to select a discipline within which to work.
- Required to address the constraints of the brief, especially noting the emphasis on the big issues and the specific requirements of that discipline, as they are different across the art and design options.

3 Individual responses with brief notes of the client information that might include the points below, for example:

(a) Client: Cancer Research UK – consider:
- history and culture, products and services, customers and market
- current designs and use of media such as websites and advertising
- legal, ethical and any environmental factors that apply.

(b) Purpose: what does the client wish to achieve?
- Increase participation and support of two target groups in its 'big issues'.
- Stronger high street presence and further develop social media for communication and fundraising.
- To launch a campaign targeting these groups through nationwide projects and events in high streets and hospitals throughout the summer months.

(c) Audience: who are the target groups and what are the considerations?
- Age: 11–18 or 19–34.
- Consider likely needs and wants of the audience.
- Consider audience demographic (e.g. income, social groups, geographical locations).

(d) Outcome: what are the outcomes and how will they be produced?
- Develop a distinct identity for its visual materials and staff (e.g. literature, visual information, uniforms, props, marketing materials (physical/web based), interactive app for instant fundraising).
- Design items to provide information and support, and an identifiable brand, as well as stressing the importance of fundraising notwithstanding pressures on the target audiences' finances.
- Commission visual ideas for visual designs for the launch campaign from art and design practitioners who should produce a presentation of up to 20 slides with their ideas in response to one of the briefs.

4 Individual responses reflecting your own choices.

Managing your time and records (page 101)

1 Individual responses for listing research and preparation and managing time to achieve this. This might include the following points, for example:

- Allocate research time – studio based.
- Allocate research time – off-site or visit based.
- Select and apply research methods.
- Select and apply visual recording.
- Allow time for initial ideas generation.
- Conduct a review of initial ideas, and action planning any further research or recording required.
- Further ideas generation.
- Select materials, techniques and processes to assist in the development of final idea.
- Use these as the rows for the Gantt chart.

2 Individual responses for ways of recording research findings both visually and in written format might include the following to complete the mind map, for example:

Organising research:
- use of headings to keep research in order
- background information on client, from visits and research
- information on chosen discipline, relating to context of brief
- visual examples of client branding, logo
- annotation of examples from discipline, e.g. uniform, shopfront

Using recording techniques:
- drawing techniques, e.g. of processes, set-ups and visualising ideas
- annotation, to critically analyse work, noting ideas and planning future ideas
- use of photography to record specific details, visits, off-site
- use of interviews and making notes in discussions
- making illustrations, concept designs
- use of diagrams to represent design development in terms of ideas, sources, and possible materials, techniques and processes.

Planning your response (page 102)
1–3 Individual responses reflecting the choice of big issue, client's requirements and audience needs.

Understanding client requirements (page 103)
Individual responses, depending on the client. If relating to the Cancer Research UK brief, responses might include the points below, for example.
1 Three benefits or outcomes the client wants to achieve from the brief, beyond the big issues:
    1 The client wants to encourage people to be more aware of the different types of cancer.
    2 Increasing research into treating cancer.
    3 Campaigning for better cancer services in the UK.
2 The personality of Cancer Research UK as a charity might include: proactive and friendly, while at the same time being highly motivated and empowering people; dynamic, professional body spearheading the drive for increased research; visible high street identity with the welfare of people at its core.
3 Individual responses reflecting the selected audience, big issue and possible product.

Researching audience needs (page 104)
1–3 Individual research reflecting the choice of audience and their characteristics, and ways of responding to the brief that takes account of their needs.

Analysing audience needs (page 105)
1–3 Individual responses reflecting the choice of organisation and audience, and ways to measure and compare how organisations meet the target audience needs.

Connecting with the audience (page 106)
1–2 Individual responses reflecting the choice of organisation and audience, and ways to test out some points from analysis, exploring starting points for initial ideas.

Visual requirements and constraints (pages 107–108)
1 Individual responses that might include the following points to complete the mind map, for example:

Symbols
- cross-cultural
- easily recognisable
- works on small and large scale
- reflects ethos of organisation

Colours
- branding colours
- can compete for attention on high street shopfront
- not copying or using other companies' colours
- works well in black and white and colour

House style
- clear accessible language, avoiding slang, to communicate

key ideas and messages
- appropriate images that clarify meaning, taking account of permission and royalty considerations
- reflecting any budgetary constraints, i.e. limited colour to reduce printing costs on publicity, stationery
- reflects the company mission and identity

Technical and other elements
- sustainability
- ethics
- multi-cultural
- non-gender specific

2 Individual responses for two pieces of visual information based on chosen organisation and pathway.

Generating and selecting ideas (pages 109–110)
1–4 Individual responses and selection reflecting the selected organisation, big issue, target audience and idea.

Refining and justifying an idea (page 111)
1–2 Individual responses reflecting the selected organisation, big issue, target audience and idea.

Reviewing the development process (pages 112–113)
1–3 Individual responses reflecting the selected organisation, big issue, target audience and idea.

Presenting a response to a client brief (pages 114–117)

Page 114
Individual responses reflecting the selected organisation, big issue, target audience and idea.
1 When considering factors that may determine how you select imagery for your slides, points might include the following, for example:
    1 Shows the way key visual information was incorporated.
    2 Shows how research informed ideas generation.
    3 Shows creative flair in initial ideas generation – generating a wide range of options.
    4 Shows the specific points that addressed the chosen big issue.
    5 Shows refinement of design ideas and the ability to select effectively.
2 Individual responses.
3 Individual responses.

Page 115
4 Four reasons why this is a weaker slide might include the following:
    1 The presentation is poor.
    2 The slide isn't named or clear.
    3 The work is poorly laid out.
    4 The work is weak and the slide doesn't provide any information about the work.

Page 116
5 Four reasons why this is a strong slide might include the following:
    1 The slide is clearly named and numbered in sequence, showing its content.
    2 The presentation and layout are strong and well balanced.
    3 The work explores the theme and is as the slide title says – refining layout ideas.
    4 It contains information about the corporate colours and evidence of review, e.g. formal elements, symbols.

Page 117
6 Individual responses.

Planning a professional presentation (pages 118–120)
1 Individual responses reflecting the selected organisation, big issue, target audience and idea. The following sequence could be considered and varied according to choices:
    1 defining the client and brief, and big issue
    2 target audience, relevant demographics, constraints
    3 researching client – research methods
    4 addressing the big issue
    5 time planning and relevant visuals, i.e. Gantt chart

6   visual sources
7   visual recording 1
8   visual recording 2
9   contextual research 1 – relevant trends within contemporary practice
10 contextual research 2 – art and design influences
11 identifying own contextual influences, i.e. technology, media communication, and so on.
12 initial ideas and visuals
13 exploring formal elements
14 mid-point review
15 action planning as result of review
16 refining idea
17 selecting materials, techniques, processes
18 testing and reviewing final idea
19 evaluating response to brief, in terms of own strengths and weaknesses
20 final art and design idea – how it successfully answers the client's brief

Presenting ideas with explanations (pages 121–122)

Individual responses reflecting the selected organisation, big issue, target audience, idea and sequence of slides.

1   Four things your speaker notes might contain and communicate might include the following:
    (a) Reinforcing the point about how a design idea uses brand colours to meet client requirements.
    (b) How you used specific contextual research to help you develop an initial idea.
    (c) How you refined an idea and what influenced you to make this revision; what information you used to inform your decision-making.
    (d) How you feel you have effectively addressed the big issue you selected, in terms of your idea and what it communicates.

2   Text summarised into notes that can be used as support for writing speaker notes:
    • Initially difficult to get going so just had to start playing around.
    • Developed some basic sort of ideas for layouts.
    • Explored the visuals I had by playing around in software.
    • Then printed out and used a mix of mark making and drawing to play around.
    • Had to try to show the company ethos but wanted to do it in a subtle way.
    • Looked at molecular designs, and developed some research based on this.
    • Links to scientific work the organisation does.
    • Could be used in logo or corporate ID; can play around with colour and layout to develop.

3   Speaker notes: example extract of a slide outline and what is important to include:
    • Key points of brief were to address big issue selected – e.g. affecting lifestyles.
    • Addressed this through targeted research of past and present campaigns based on public health.
    • Worked up a series of proposal ideas based on in-depth research on what would make effective campaign.
    • Carried out contextual research into current trends on health awareness campaigns globally.
    • The final idea should be effective in reaching target audience as it would feature strong visuals to communicate message.
    • Meets client needs as addresses key big issue lifestyle choices.
    • Follows all corporate house styles re images and text.
    • Reinforces Cancer Research UK brand and mission in a positive way.
    • Is both a plea to adopt change and a warning of what may happen if ignored.
    • Consider it to be a powerful set of images and text.

Revision activity

Revision activity 1 (page 123)

Individual responses that should be assessed against the criteria noted.

Unit 7: Developing and Realising Creative Intentions

Interpreting a brief (pages 131–132)

1   Individual responses to summarise requirements of the revision task brief that might include the points below, for example:
    • selecting the discipline for the response
    • defining and understanding the theme
    • a plan for research, identifying primary and secondary sources
    • recording information from research in an annotated log, including samples and visuals
    • researching contextual trends and current work to help you locate your work within contemporary practice
    • annotated examples of research and critical thinking
    • ideas for the proposal, to include initial ideas for the piece and reasoning
    • time plan including resources and any specialist assistance
    • specialist techniques, materials and processes
    • ideas on how to approach the design development process, including tests, samples, models and mock-ups
    • ideas on ensuring you work through the realisation stage and complete on time
    • how review will be used to select examples of work to record for your digital portfolio
    • how you can explain and demonstrate the stages in your design development, including refinement
    • examples of review, analysis and evaluation of your work, and action planning.

2   Individual responses to summarise the revision task information that might include the below, for example:
    • Theme is structure.
    • It can be interpreted in different ways.
    • The information contains starting points from which ideas and a response can be developed.
    • The theme can be interpreted in a way that links to a chosen specialist pathway or discipline.
    • There are a series of images, definitions, a quotation and prompts that can be used to kick-start the ideas generation process.
    • There are visual clues in some of the images.
    • There is also a list of artists and designers that can be used as a basis to plan initial contextual research.
    • The work in this unit should also be referenced against contemporary practice in the discipline.

3   Individual responses.

Planning a response (page 133)

1–3   Individual responses. You should consider possible starting points and select and explain ideas, when planning a response.

Exploring and recording sources (pages 134-135)

1–4   Individual responses. You should research and make records that reflect the choice of initial ideas.

Generating ideas (page 136)

1   Individual responses. You should generate and explain two initial ideas.

Developing and recording ideas (pages 137–138)

1–2   Individual responses. You should make plans to develop and record ideas from research to production.

Experimenting with ideas (page 139)

1   Individual responses. You should experiment with ideas and test them out.

Experimenting with Ms, Ts and Ps (pages 140–141)
1–2 Individual responses. You should experiment and explain choices in relation to a selected idea.

Influences of practitioners on ideas (page 142)
1–2 Individual responses. You should deconstruct and communicate the influence of chosen artists and designers on your own work and practice, and on trends.

Contextual influences on ideas (pages 143–144)
1–2 Individual responses for art and design and non-art and design contextual research, reflecting your choices.

Planning your proposal (pages 145–146)
1–6 Individual responses reflecting your proposal to create a piece of art and design in a discipline of your choice, with a clear purpose.

Identifying scope and timescales (page 147)
1 Individual responses reflecting your choices.

Developing contextual research (page 148)
1–2 Individual responses for developing contextual research, reflecting your practical work.

Recording work in progress (pages 149–150)
1 Individual responses. Two benefits of using written description and photography to record a process and demonstrate a work in progress might include the following, for example:
   (a) Written description can be used to describe the key stages in the process, and clarify sequence of events or activities.
   (b) Photography can be used to accurately show parts of a complicated process, and can be used together with text to make a thorough and detailed record.
2 Individual responses for how the idea is developing from image 1 to image 4 might include the following, for example:
   Image 1: Colour is naturalistic, tonal range established objects closer to viewer, composition based on uprights and simple horizontal division.
   Image 2: Colours heightened in central lower area with pale purple, reds added to right and some uprights, creates more dramatic effect and contrast, forms still readable as trees.
   Image 3: Image simplified, individual tree uprights simplified into brush marks of colour, pale pink and white added to distance, creates higher lighting, greens added to tree forms, brush marks are left evident, image is becoming flattened with less depth.
   Image 4: Brighter green added, pinks overpainted in mint green, some changes to uprights and horizontals, image now even more like a flattened design or arrangement of colours and shapes, progressively less depth, i.e. than in image 3.

Exploring development through the production process (page 151)
1 Individual responses. You should reflect ways that you explore and evaluate effectiveness through the production process.

Reviewing and refining ideas (page 152)
1–2 Individual responses. You should review and refine ideas and practical work based on your planning, proposal and production process.

Reflecting on progress (page 153)
1 Individual responses. Factors might include the following from sample response extracts:
   Describing the way marks have been used in this image: The mark making uses darker colours on top of the lighter background to show details in some areas, and to emphasise some of the characteristics in the scene.
   Describing the effect of the mark making: The overall effect of the mark making seems to emphasise the horizontal movement or ripples in the water, in a slightly expressive though still naturalistic way as it is following the lines the water would take, but is made with direct marks that show energy.
   Comparing the two images and describing how the colour in this image is different, and where it remained the same: The colour remains the same in the foliage of the treeline on the left, and in parts of the water; it is similar though slightly

adapted in the treeline on the right; it is radically different in the treatment of the sky.
   Explaining the effect of the colour range on this image, for example to communicate a 'mood' or a different feeling to the other image: The first image has a more naturalistic mood, and could be a view of a typical scene; the second image has heightened colour and a much more dramatic sky, which gives the whole image more contrast; the different parts of the image now stand out more, for instance the church is now much more visible, as lighter than surrounding sky.

Planning to adapt or change (page 154)
1 Individual responses that reflect choices for improvement.

Completing final piece to deadline (page 155)
1 Individual responses that reflect the final piece of work and specialism.

Realising your final piece of work (page 156)
1 Individual responses that reflect the final piece of work with a clear purpose, in a specialism of your choice, that meets the brief.

Producing a portfolio (pages 157–158)
1 Three factors that may determine how you select imagery and annotation that shows your **creative response to the theme**:
   (a) To show a wide range of ideas generation.
   (b) To show how materials, techniques and processes, used in exciting ways, have been selected.
   (c) To show the plan for the creative journey through the brief.
2 Three factors that may determine how you select imagery and annotation that shows your use of **contextual sources and influences** in your work:
   (a) To show the specific contextual examples and sources used and how they relate to the theme.
   (b) To show depth and understanding of contextual factors and current trends.
   (c) To demonstrate visual deconstruction and analysis, used to support the development process, supporting and justifying conclusions reached.
3 Three factors that may determine how you select imagery and annotation that shows your **exploration of materials, techniques and processes** in your development work:
   (a) To show examples of tests, samples, maquettes, models, mock-ups, roughs.
   (b) To show exploration of materials, techniques and processes in the experimental phase of development process.
   (c) To demonstrate how specialist processes have been used.
4 Three factors that may determine your selection of imagery and annotation that shows how you **refine your work through review and evaluation**:
   (a) To show critical reflection through comment and annotation.
   (b) To show imagery that demonstrates development and refinement through selection of appropriate materials, techniques and processes.
   (c) To show the review process and how this has refined development.
5 Three factors that may determine your selection of imagery and annotation that allows your portfolio to show well all the **development and realisation processes**:
   (a) To make sure all the stages in the development process are equally presented.
   (b) To show the stages in development process sequentially, to demonstrate a consistent and coherent approach and clear progression.
   (c) To make sure relevant annotation and action planning is clearly recorded.
6 Three factors that may determine the quality of **presentation of the portfolio**:
   (a) To take care when mounting any work.
   (b) To use any digital editing software carefully and consistently to control image exposure, contrast and so on.
   (c) To ensure final outcomes are recorded with care and well presented.
7 Individual response.

Recording images for a portfolio (pages 159–160)

1 Individual responses.
2 Individual responses.
3 Responses for ensuring that all images are well lit and clear might include the following:
   - Use a studio space if possible, and light the subject equally across its surface.
   - Use controlled lighting – either studio or natural without direct sunlight or shadow.
   - Use a good quality camera and accessories, and use the controls effectively.
   - Practise recording the subjects to see how the lighting affects them.
   - Use editing software to correct any issues.
4 Individual responses.

Planning a written commentary (pages 161–163)

1–3 Individual responses for planning a written commentary might reflect the factors below, for example:

Page 1: definition of theme, clear purpose, chosen specialism
Page 2: initial research, examples of primary and secondary research
Page 3: examples of visual recording and initial ideas generation, materials exploration
Page 4: project planning and ideas for inclusion in proposal
Page 5: diagram showing key points from proposal, and actions, including time planning
Page 6: examples of further research, showing understanding of contextual factors and current trends
Page 7: initial review, including examples of refinement, ideas generation, using visual recording and other sources
Page 8: final idea in art and design format according to discipline, i.e. concept drawing, presentation board, model and so on
Page 9: materials exploration, including tests, samples, mock-ups, maquettes, roughs
Page 10: studies, evidence of review of experimental phase, ongoing review and annotation of the work against the theme, including target setting for production phase
Page 11: initial production stage, showing links to results of review
Page 12: mid-point in production phase, showing any use of specialist techniques, materials and processes
Page 13: final production phase, including evidence of refinement in use of techniques, materials and processes
Page 14: final piece(s)
Page 15: summary of key stages in development process including images
Page 16: final evaluation, including how outcome meets the brief

Revision activities

Revision activity 2 (pages 164–165)

Individual responses that should be assessed against the criteria noted.

Revision activity 5 (page 166)

Individual responses that should be assessed against the criteria noted.

Notes

Notes

Notes

Notes